MY FAMILY'S FAVORITES

By Mary Beth Roe, QVC Host

Published by FLP Publications
Post Office Box 208
Long Prairie, Minnesota 56347

Sold exclusively through QVC Network   1-800-345-1515   Item No. K-2237

ACKNOWLEDGEMENTS

I've sent out hundreds of recipes each month to viewers who watch my cook shows. About 75% of my mail asks me when I'm coming out with a cookbook. After six-and-a-half years of being in the cable shopping business, I decided it was time to put all of my family's favorite recipes in one book so that all of you can enjoy them, too. These recipes are easy to make and I promise they taste good, too! I wanted to give you recipes that you can make on a daily basis, as well as for entertaining and for holidays. There are even a few Scandinavian recipes, since my heritage is Swedish and Norwegian.

Many, many thanks go to Mom and Dad for teaching me how to cook and sharing many of their great recipes with me for this book. Many thanks also go to my sisters Sharon, Faith and Diane for their terrific recipes and all the cooking tips they've given me over the years. My parents and my entire family have always been so loving and supportive. They are my biggest fans and I thank them for everything!

I also want to say thank you to both Virginia Olson and Helen Chen, who frequently appear on QVC and have taught me many things about being a good cook.

I really want to thank my loving husband for his constant support and encouragement and for always being willing to try my new recipes and for being patient with me while I learned to cook decently. He's always eaten what I put in front of him and never complained. He reached for more ketchup many times, but never complained! I love him more than anyone in the world!!

Most importantly, I thank my Lord Jesus Christ for the many blessings He has bestowed on me, including my family, my job and the many people who have come into my life.

I hope you enjoy this book. Eat well and God Bless You!!

Mary Beth Roe

TABLE OF CONTENTS

Appetizers & Beverages

Onion-Cheese Dip Mix

1 Tbsp. minced onion
1 Tbsp. parmesan cheese
1 1/2 instant beef bouillon

1/2 tsp. garlic salt
1 c. sour cream

Mix together and refrigerate for several hours. Serve with crackers.

Shrimply Divine Dip

8 oz. cream cheese, softened
1 cup sour cream
2 tsp. lemon juice

1 - 5/8 oz. pkg. Italian salad dressing mix
2 cans chopped shrimp, drained

Blend cream cheese with the rest of the ingredients. Chill one hour. Great with fresh vegetables, chips, and small crackers.

Clam Dip for Vegies

16 oz. cream cheese
16 oz. sour cream
2 cans minced clams, drained

2 Tbsp. barbeque sauce
2 Tbsp. grated onion

Cream cheese until smooth. Mix with rest of ingredients and refrigerate. Serve with raw vegetables.

Curry Dip for Vegetables

1 cup real mayonnaise
1/2 tsp. chili powder
1 tsp. curry powder

1 tsp. Worcestershire Sauce
grated onion or chives to taste

Mix together and chill.

Raw Vegetable Dip

1 cup sour cream with chives
1 tsp. parsley flakes
1 tsp. seasoned salt

1 cup mayonnaise
1/2 cup parmesan cheese
1 tsp. garlic salt

Combine all ingredients and refrigerate overnight. Serve with assorted fresh vegetables.

Spinach Dip

10 oz. pkg. frozen chopped spinach
16 oz. sour cream

1 cup mayonnaise (not salad dressing)
1 pkg. dry vegetable soup mix

Thaw and drain spinach, squeezing out excess moisture. Mix all ingredients together and refrigerate 3 to 4 hours. Hollow out a loaf of round, unsliced rye or sourdough bread. Put dip in center of bread and pieces of bread from center of loaf around outside of plate for dipping.

Fruit Dip

7 oz. jar marshmallow creme
8 oz. cream cheese
1/4 tsp. nutmeg

1/4 tsp. cinnamon
1/2 tsp. vanilla

Mix ingredients together and stir until smooth. Serve with all kinds of fruit (sliced bananas, apple slices, mandarin oranges, pineapple chunks, etc.)

Almond Chantilly Strawberry Dip

3 oz. box instant vanilla pudding
1 cup heavy cream, whipped

1 tsp. almond extract

Prepare pudding mix according to package directions. Fold in almond extract and whipped cream. Serve with fresh strawberries.

Reuben Dip

8 oz. cream cheese
1 1/2 cup sour cream, softened
12 oz. shredded Swiss cheese

15 oz. can saurkraut, drained
8 oz. corned beef, chopped

Mix all ingredients together and warm on medium power in microwave until cheese melts (not too hot; do it slowly.) Serve with rye crackers or pumpernickle bread.

Sweet and Sour Dip

3 Tbsp. vinegar
4 Tbsp. sugar
4 Tbsp. ketchup

3 tsp. cornstarch
1 tsp. salt
1/4 cup water (or more)

Combine cornstarch and water and blend until smooth; add remaining ingredients. Mix together; heat until thickens.   May be served hot or cold. Great with Egg Rolls.

Taco Dip

8 oz. cream cheese
12 oz. cottage cheese, small curd
1/4 cup sour cream
1 pkg. taco seasoning

shredded cheddar cheese
shredded lettuce
chopped tomatoes
tostada chips

Combine cream cheese, cottage cheese, sour cream and taco seasoning. Blend together with electric mixer. Spread mixture onto a serving plate. Cover with shredded lettuce, then a layer of chopped tomatoes and lastly the shredded cheese.   Serve with chips.

Hot Taco Dip

1 lb. lean ground beef
1 medium onion, chopped
8 oz. jar taco sauce
1 tsp. Worcestershire sauce
1/2 tsp. chili powder
1/4 tsp. seasoned salt

3 taco shells, crushed
2 cups shredded lettuce
2 tomatoes, peeled and chopped
4 oz. can chopped green chilies
4 oz. shredded cheddar cheese
corn chips

In a T-FAL 3 quart sauce pan, cook ground beef and onion over medium heat until browned; drain. Stir in taco sauce, Worcestershire sauce, chili powder and seasoned salt. Reduce heat and simmer for 8-10 minutes. Add crushed taco shells, lettuce, tomatoes, chilies and cheese. Stir gently to blend. Serve with corn chips for dipping.

Mexican Dip

2 cans bean dip, regular or jalapeno
1 cup mayonnaise
1 cup sour cream
1 pkg. taco seasoning

shredded cheese
chopped tomatoes
black olives, sliced
chopped green onion tips

Mix bean dip, mayonnaise, sour cream and taco seasoning. Spread on a serving plate. Top with remaining ingredients.

Dried Beef Dip

1 pkg. dried beef, chopped
1/3 cup green pepper, finely chopped
1/4 cup chopped onion
8 oz. cream cheese, softened

16 oz. sour cream
1 tsp. garlic powder
2 tsp. milk
chopped pecans

Mix together all ingredients except pecans. Bake in small baking dish at 300 degrees for 15-20 minutes. Top with pecans. Serve with crackers.

Ranch Dressing Cheese Ball

1 pkg. Ranch Dressing mix
1/2 cup mayonnaise
1/2 cup milk

8 oz. cheddar cheese, shredded
6 oz. cream cheese, softened
5 oz. sliced almonds, roasted

Combine the ranch dressing mix, mayonnaise and milk. Mix well. (This will actually make a double-strength salad dressing.) Use 1/2 cup of this dressing mix, blend with cream cheese, and beat well with electric mixer. Add cheddar cheese and blend. Cover and freeze for 30 minutes. Shape cheese mixture into a ball. Roll cheese ball in roasted almonds.

Cheese Ball

16 oz. cream cheese
2 small jars New England Sharp
    Cheese Spread

1 Tbsp. worcestershire sauce
1 small onion, chopped

Mix together and chill until firm. Shape unto a ball and top with chopped nuts and parsley flakes.

Cheese Spread on Crackers

1 1/2 cup mayonnaise
2 cups shredded mozzarella cheese
2 cups shredded cheddar cheese

1 can ripe olives, pitted and chopped
6 green onions, chopped
Triscuit crackers (or cracker of your choice)

Combine all ingredients except crackers. Put a spoonful of cheese mixture on each cracker and put crackers on a cookie sheet. Bake at 250 degrees for 15-20 minutes. Serve hot. Yield: 5 dozen

Golden Cheese Bites

8 oz. natural brick, muenster or Monterey
    Jack cheese
2 eggs, beaten
1/2 cup grated parmesan cheese

1/2 cup dry bread crumbs
1/2 tsp. onion salt
oil

Cut brick cheese into 24 cubes. Dip in egg; coat with combined parmesan cheese, crumbs and onion salt. Repeat. Fry in deep oil, 375 degrees, until lightly browned. To Make Ahead: Cover uncooked appetizers; refrigerate. When ready to serve, fry as directed.

Hot Cheese Balls

1/2 lb. grated parmesan cheese
1/2 lb. cream cheese, softened
2 eggs

dash cayenne
1 cup bread crumbs
peanut or salad oil for frying

In medium bowl, combine both kinds of cheese, the eggs and cayenne. Beat with wooden spoon until smooth. Form into 1 1/4-inch balls. Roll each lightly in bread crumbs on waxed paper. Refrigerate. In a deep skillet or deep-fat fryer, slowly heat oil, about 2 inches, to 350 degrees. Fry cheese balls, turning once, 1 minute or until golden brown. Drain on paper towels. Serve hot. Makes 24.

Cheese-Stuffed Bread

1/2 cup mayonnaise
1 cup grated sharp cheddar cheese
3/4 cup finely chopped green onion
few drops worcestershire sauce

1 loaf French bread (about 20-inches long)
paprika
10 pimento-stuffed green olives
toothpicks

Heat oven to 350 degrees. Mix mayonnaise, cheese, green onions and worcestershire sauce. Cut a slit length-wise down center of French bread, being careful not to cut through the bottom crust. Spread cheese mixture in slit in bread; sprinkle with paprika. Wrap bread in foil, leaving the top open. Bake 20 to 25 minutes, until cheese is melted and bread is hot. Remove and discard foil. Cut bread into 2-inch-wide slices; garnish each with a stuffed olive impaled on a wooden pick. Serve hot. Makes 10 slices.

Cheese and Mushroom Appetizers

8 oz. finely chopped mushrooms
2 Tbsp. butter or margarine
1/2 tsp. garlic salt
2 Tbsp. minced onion
1 tsp. lemon juice

1 tsp. worcestershire sauce
8 oz. pkg. crescent rolls
6 oz. cream cheese, softened
1/4 cup grated parmesan cheese

Brown mushrooms, onion, butter, garlic salt, lemon juice and worcestershire sauce. Cook until all liquid is evaporated. Pat out crescent rolls into a well-greased 9x13-inch pan. Spread cream cheese over dough and sprinkle parmesan cheese over that. Spread browned ingredients over the cheese and bake for 20 minutes at 350 degrees. Cut into squares. Serve hot.

Toasted Cubes

1 loaf French bread
8 oz. cream cheese
1/2 lb. sharp cheddar cheese, grated

1/2 lb. margarine
4 egg whites, stiffly beaten

Remove crust from French bread and cut into 1-inch squares. In double boiler, melt cheeses and margarine. When creamy, fold in beaten egg whites. Dip cubes into mixture and place on a waxed-paper lined cookie sheet and freeze. When frozen, place in a plastic bag and store in freezer. To serve, bake frozen cubes at 450 degrees for about 8 minutes. Serve warm. These taste so good!

Mushroom Deviled Eggs

6 hard-cooked eggs
1/4 cup sour cream (or plain yogurt)
1/2 tsp. dill weed
1/8 tsp. salt

1/4 cup finely chopped fresh mushrooms
2 Tbsp. minced green onions
fresh mushroom slices, optional
fresh dill sprigs, optional

Cut eggs in half lengthwise. Remove yolks and set whites aside. Mash yolks with fork. Blend in sour cream and seasonings. Gently stir in mushrooms and onions. Refill whites using about 1 Tbsp. yolk mixture for each egg half. Garnish with mushroom slices and dill sprigs, if desired.

Delicious Deviled Eggs

1 dozen hard boiled eggs
1/4 cup Hellmans Dijonaise (substitute
     with mustard if unavailable)
1/4 cup Hellmans real mayonnaise
1/4 cup Miracle Whip salad dressing

ground onion, fresh or dried
garlic powder
salt
pepper
paprika

Peel and rinse eggs. Separate into halves by slicing each egg lengthwise. Put egg yolks into medium mixing bowl. Use a fork to mash yolks in bowl until most of the chunks are gone. Add dijonaise, mayonnaise and salad dressing until you reach desired texture (about 1/4 cup of each.) Add onion, garlic powder, salt and pepper to your taste. Fill egg whites with mixture, about 1 Tbsp. per egg half. Sprinkle top of finished eggs with paprika. Serve chilled. (This recipe was given to me by Gina Francesco from Fancy Faces Make-Up.)

Party Bread

1 round loaf of bread
swiss cheese
mushrooms

1/2 cup butter or margarine, melted
garlic powder

Cut through the loaf of bread, in strips, about 3/4 of the way from top to bottom. Make strips about 1/2 inch wide. Then slice the bread crosswise to your first cuts, same width as before, making a checkerboard effect. Fill the cracks you have made in the bread with swiss cheese and mushrooms. Pour the melted butter over the top, allowing the melted butter to run down in the cracks . Sprinkle garlic powder over the top. Wrap in foil. Bake at 350 degrees for about 20 minutes.

Snack Bread

8 oz. cream cheese
1 pkg. ranch dressing mix

cocktail rye bread slices
1 cucumber, peeled and sliced

Mix cream cheese and ranch dressing mix until well blended. Spread on cocktail rye bread slices, place a slice of cucumber on top of each slice of bread and sprinkle with dill weed on top, if desired.

Vegetable Pizza

1 pkg. crescent rolls
8 oz. cream cheese, softened
1/3 cup real mayonnaise
1/2 tsp. dill weed
1/2 tsp. garlic powder
1 tsp. minced onion

any combination of chopped, raw
  vegetables:
cauliflower, broccoli, green peppers
  (diced), green onions (chopped),
  cucumbers, grated carrots, tomatoes
  (diced), olives

Spread crescent roll on greased pizza pan. Pat down. Bake for 8 to 10 minutes at 375 degrees; cool. Blend mayonnaise, cream cheese, dill weed, garlic powder and onion and spread on crust. Put on vegetables desired. Sprinkle with grated cheese over all.

Fruit Pizza

1/2 cup butter
1 cup flour
1/4 cup powdered sugar
8 oz. cream cheese, softened
1/3 cup sugar
1 tsp. vanilla
3 Tbsp. cornstarch

fruit (strawberries, chunk pineapple, kiwi,
   blueberries, seedless grapes, diced apples
   with peelings, bananas (dip in glaze first)
1 1/2 cup juice (from pineapple; add water,
   if needed)
3/4 cup sugar
1 1/2 tsp. lemon juice

Grease a round 14-inch pizza pan. Mix butter, flour and powdered sugar and pat in pan. Bake at 350 degrees for 15 minutes. Watch closely! Cool. Beat cream cheese, 1/3 cup sugar and vanilla until blended. Spread on cooled crust. Arrange fruit: strawberries around outside, the remaining fruit in the middle. Combine juice, cornstarch, 3/4 cup sugar and lemon juice. Heat until thickens. Pour this glaze over top of fruit while hot.

Bacon Squares

1 cup mayonnaise or salad dressing
2 tsp. worcestershire sauce
1/2 tsp. salad seasoning
1/4 tsp. paprika
2 cups shredded cheddar cheese

8 slices bacon, crisply fried and crumbled
1/3 cup chopped peanuts
4 green onions, sliced (1/4 cup)
14 slices white bread

Heat oven to 400 degrees. Mix mayonnaise, worcestershire sauce, salad seasoning, and paprika. Stir in cheese, bacon, peanuts and onions. Spread about 3 Tbsp. bacon mixture over each slice of bread. Bake on ungreased baking sheet 10 minutes. Cut each slice into 4 pieces. Serve hot. 56 appetizers.

Egg Rolls

1 lb. hamburger
1 lb. cabbage, chopped
1 carrot, grated
1/4 cup onion, chopped

2 Tbsp. soy sauce
1/2 tsp. salt
1 tsp. cornstarch mixed with 1 Tbsp. water
pkg. egg roll wrappers

Brown hamburger with onion; drain. Add cabbage and grated carrot. Cook until tender. Add soy sauce, salt and cornstarch; simmer 5 minutes. Fill egg roll wrappers with 2 to 3 Tbsp. filling. Make paste of flour and water and spread on edge of egg roll wrapper to seal shut. Fry in 350 degree oil. Serve with Sweet and Sour Dip.

Fruit Cup

6 oz. can frozen orange juice concentrate
6 oz. can frozen lemonade concentrate
10 oz. frozen strawberries
1 small jar maraschino cherries

3 bananas, sliced
1 lb. can crushed pineapple
3 cups water
1/2 cup sugar

Mix orange juice and lemonade concentrate with 3 cups water and 1/2 cup sugar. Add strawberries, cherries, bananas and pineapple. Spoon into empty 5-quart ice cream pail and freeze. Take out about 2 hours before serving. Yield: 10 cups or 20 - 1/2 cup servings. Note: you can also add fresh blueberries in season.

Glazed Fruit and Franks

1 small jar apricot preserves
1/3 cup lemon juice
1 Tbsp. cornstarch
1/2 tsp. cinnamon
1 can pineapple chunks, drained

1 pkg. cocktail frankfurters, or
    8 oz. frankfurters cut into 1-inch pieces
1 large red apple, cored and cut into chunks
1 large can mandarin orange segments

In saucepan, combine preserves, lemon juice, cornstarch and cinnamon. Cook and stir until well blended and slightly thickened. Stir in frankfurters and pineapple; heat through. Just before serving, stir in apples and oranges. Serve warm.

Fancy Franks on Rye

10 oz. miniature frankfurters
1/2 cup pimento cheese spread

16 slices rye or pumpernickel slices,
    cut in half crosswise

With a sharp knife, cut frankfurters almost through, making from 16 to 18 slices on each frankfurter. (It will look a little like a miniature slinky.) Spread 1/2 tsp. of cheese spread on each half slice of bread. Put one frankfurter on each slice of bread, curving it slightly. Place on rack in broiler pan, four inches from heat, and broil 10 to 12 minutes.

Sweet and Sour Chicken Wings

24 chicken wings, cut in half and
   cut off tips
1 cup sugar
1 cup soy sauce
1 cup water

1/2 cup salad oil
1/4 cup frozen concentrate pineapple juice
1 tsp. ginger
1 tsp. garlic salt

Mix all ingredients except chicken wings. Marinate chicken wings in sauce for 48 hours. Stir occasionally. To bake, spread on foil covered cookie sheet. Bake 1 hour at 350 degrees.

Cocktail Meatballs

1 lb. lean hamburger
1/4 lb. pork sausage
1/4 cup dry bread crumbs
1 egg
1/2 cup parmesan cheese
10 oz. grape jelly

12 oz. chili sauce
1 Tbsp. Worcestershire sauce
1/2 tsp. garlic salt
1/8 tsp. pepper
1/4 cup light cream

Mix hamburger, sausage, bread crumbs, egg and parmesan cheese; form into 1-inch diameter meatballs. Brown in skillet until cooked through. In separate saucepan, melt the grape jelly on low heat; add chili sauce, Worcestershire sauce and remaining ingredients. Heat and combine with meatballs. Serve warm. Makes approx. 40 one-inch meatballs.

Crab Canapes

6 oz. pkg. frozen crabmeat, thawed and
   drained or 1 can crabmeat, drained
1 Tbsp. chopped green onion
1 cup shredded Swiss cheese
1/2 cup mayonnaise

1/4 tsp. curry powder
1/2 tsp. salt
1 tsp. lemon juice
8 oz. pkg. butterflake refrigerator rolls
8 oz. can water chestnuts, drained & sliced

Preheat oven to 400 degrees. Grease a baking sheet. In medium bowl, combine crab, onion, cheese, mayonnaise, curry powder, salt and lemon juice. Mix well. Separate each roll into 3 layers, making 36 pieces. Place pieces on baking sheet. Spoon a small amount of mixture on each piece. Top with slice of water chestnut. Bake 12 minutes until puffed and brown. Serve hot. May be frozen and reheated.

Crab Melts

1 lb. crabmeat
12 oz. grated sharp cheddar cheese
1 cup butter

4 Tbsp. mayonnaise
1 tsp. salt

Mix all ingredients except crabmeat; then fold in crabmeat. Spread on top of 1/4 pieces of English muffins. Broil until browned. Serve warm.

Poppin' Party Mix

4 cups Quaker Corn Bran cereal
1 1/2 cups pretzel sticks
1 cup salted peanuts

1/3 cup margarine or butter, melted
1/4 cup grated parmesan cheese
1 tsp. onion powder

Heat oven to 300 degrees. In large bowl, combine cereal, pretzels and peanuts. Pour melted butter over cereal mixture, mixing well. Sprinkle with cheese and onion powder; toss well to coat. Spread into ungreased 15x10-inch jelly roll pan. Bake 20 to 25 minutes, or until deep golden brown, stirring occasionally during baking.

Egg Nog

4 eggs, beaten
1/2 cup sugar

1 tsp. vanilla
1 quart milk

Mix in blender or with beater.

Christmas Eggnog Punch

12 eggs
3/4 cup sugar
10 cups water
48 oz. frozen orange juice

1 cup lemon juice
1/2 gallon vanilla ice cream
2 quarts ginger ale

Beat eggs and sugar until lemon-colored. Sitr in water, melted orange juice and lemon juice. Place scoops of ice cream in punch bowl. Pour egg-juice mixture over ice cream. Just before serving, add ginger ale. A festive, delicious Christmas Eve treat with hors d'oeuvres. Make about 32 punch-cup size servings.

Smoothie

2-3 cups fresh or frozen fruit of your
　　choice (strawberries, bananas, grapes,
　　oranges, pears)

fruit juice
1/2 cup yogurt
1/2 tsp. vanilla or almond extract

Cover fruit with fruit juice (orange, pineapple, grape). Add remaining ingredients. Blend all together until smooth. Makes 2 to 4 servings.

Sweetheart Berry-Berry

1 pint raspberry sherbet

2 cups cold milk

Blend together 15 seconds on high speed. Serve in tall glasses. Serves two.

Creamy Lemon Punch

2 qt. lemon sherbet
2 qt. 7-Up

1 1/2 cans apricot nectar

Chill 7-Up and nectar. Mix ingredients in punch bowl or large container. Add sherbet and mix well. Mixture will have consistency of thick shake.

Homemade Orange Julius

1 cup water
1 cup milk
1/2 cup sugar

1 tsp. vanilla
6 oz. can frozen orange juice, undiluted
8-9 ice cubes

Mix together in a blender and serve. Serves 4 or 5.

Think-Thin Coffee Milk Shake

1 cup cold skim milk
3 ice cubes

1 tsp. powdered instant coffee
artificial sweetener to taste

Combine all ingredients in blender. Blend on high for 15 seconds. Tastes like the real thing but boasts only 85 calories.

Quick Lemonade

6 1/2 cups bottled water
1 cup lemon juice

1 cup sugar

Combine ingredients; stir until sugar dissolves. Chill, if desired. Serve over ice.

Jello Punch

6 oz. pkg. jello (any flavor, depending
   on color desired)
1 1/4 cups sugar
3 1/2 cups boiling water

12 oz. frozen lemonade concentrate
46 oz. pineapple juice
6 cups cold water
2 large (2 liter) bottles 7-Up

Dissolve jello and sugar in boiling water. Stir in lemonade, pineapple juice and cold water.
Put in empty ice cream pail and freeze. Remove from freezer 5 to 6 hours ahead of serving
time. To serve, break up slush and add 7-Up. Punch will be slushy. This works great for
graduation, etc., as you can determine color of punch by the flavor of the jello. Makes 50
five-ounce servings.

Kool-Aid Punch

10 pkgs. Kool-Aid, unsweetened,
   any flavor
7 cups sugar
10 quarts water

24 oz. frozen orange juice
46 oz. pineapple juice
12 oz. frozen lemonade concentrate
4 liters ginger ale

In a large container, mix all ingredients together. Do not add ginger ale until just before
serving. I make some of the punch (or Kool-Aid of the same flavor) ahead (not including
ginger ale) and freeze in molds or plastic containers to use as large "ice cubes". This keeps
the punch cold at the event without diluting it with more water. This is good to use at
graduation open house or wedding receptions as you can determine the color of the punch
by the flavor of the Kool-Aid. It does not make a good purple-colored punch, however.
Approximately 100 five-ounce servings.

Cherry Punch

3 oz. pkg. cherry jello
1 cup boiling water
6 oz. can frozen lemonade

3 cups cold water
1 quart cranberry juice
1 quart ginger ale

Dissolve jello in boiling water. When cool, add remaining ingredients. (Ginger ale should not be added until just before serving.)

Red Punch

2 pkg. cherry or raspberry Koolaid
2 cups sugar
2 quarts water

46 oz. can pineapple juice
1 quart ginger ale (or 7-Up)
Add a little sherbet or ice cream

Fast Fruit Punch

1 quart ginger ale
46 oz. can pineapple juice
32 oz. bottle grape juice

6 oz. can frozen orange juice, prepared
6 oz. can frozen lemonade, prepared

Combine all ingredients in punch bowl. Add ice and a fresh fruit garnish. Serves 40. A great thirst-quencher and a pretty purple color.

Festive Punch

18 oz. frozen lemonade, prepared
10 oz. pkg. frozen strawberries, thawed
1 quart chilled ginger ale

ice (or ice ring)
1 pint raspberry sherbet
fresh whole raspberries

Pour lemonade into the punch bowl and stir in strawberries. Just before serving, add ginger ale and ice, then stir in sherbet. Place a raspberry in each cup and serve. Serves 10.

Quick Punch

1 quart pineapple sherbet
1 quart vanilla ice cream

24 oz. pineapple juice
36 oz. 7-Up or lemon-lime soda

Mix all ingredients in punch bowl. Makes 25-30 punch cup servings.

Best-Ever Slush Punch

46 oz. pineapple juice
46 oz. orange juice
1 cup sugar
1 cup water

30 oz. frozen Hawaiian punch concentrate
  (or 1 quart liquid concentrate)
2 quarts ginger ale

Mix all ingredients in an empty 5-quart ice cream pail. Mix well. Freeze. Take out of freezer 4-5 hours ahead to thaw a little. Chop up with a knife to make a slush. Put into punch bowl and add ginger ale just before serving. Will be slushy. Makes 50 - 5 oz. servings. (You can make this several days ahead of time and keep in freezer until a few hours before serving.)

Sunshine Slush

1/3 cup frozen orange juice concentrate
1 egg
1 tsp. vanilla

1/3 cup powdered milk
2 Tbsp. honey
6 ice cubes

Mix all together in blender, adding ice cubes one at a time. Serve immediately. Great for breakfast.

Fruit Punch

46 oz. pineapple juice
46 oz. grapefruit juice
12 oz. can frozen lemonade
12 oz. can frozen orange juice

2 oz. bottle almond flavoring
2 cups sugar
2 quarts water
2 quarts ginger ale or 7-Up

Mix together and serve.

Banana Smash

2 cups sugar
5 ripe bananas
6 cups water
2 Tbsp. concentrated lemon juice

12 oz. frozen orange juice, prepared
32 oz. unsweetened pineapple juice
2 quarts 7-Up

Mix sugar and water. Boil 5 minutes. Cool. Mash bananas and add lemon juice right away. Mix everything together, except 7-Up, and freeze. Thaw for 1 hour before serving. Add 7-Up when ready to serve.

Evergreen Punch

4 pints lime sherbet (1/2 gallon)

6 liters lemon-lime soft drink

Mix and serve. Really nice at Christmas or St. Patrick's Day!

Cranberry-Raspberry Punch

1 quart white soda
1 pint cranberry cocktail
12 oz. can frozen lemonade

12oz. can frozen pineapple-orange drink
1 quart raspberry sherbet

Mix together and serve. Serves 12-15.

Cranberry Punch

1 pint cranberry juice
1 quart apple juice
12 oz. frozen lemonade concentrate

6 oz. frozen pineapple juice concentrate
6 oz. frozen grapefruit juice concentrate
2 liters lemon-lime soda

Mix and serve.

Apple Drink

4 cups apple juice
4 cups water
1 pkg. red Kool-Aid
3/4 cup sugar

1/4 tsp. cinnamon
1/8 tsp. nutmeg
1/8 tsp. cloves

Blend all ingredients together. Serve hot or cold.

Hot Cider Drink

6 cups apple cider (46 oz.)
1 cinnamon stick
1/4 cup honey
18 oz. pineapple juice

1/4 tsp. nutmeg
3 Tbsp. lemon juice
lemon rind

Boil cider and cinnamon stick together. Add other ingredients and heat through. Serve hot.

Cranberry Hot Drink

4 cups cranberry juice
2 cups apple juice
2 cups orange juice
1/2 cup maple flavored syrup

1 tsp. cinnamon
1/2 tsp. ground nutmeg
1/2 tsp. ground cloves

Mix cranberry juice, apple juice, orange juice and syrup in 30-cup (or larger) coffee percolator. Put cinnamon, nutmeg and cloves in percolator basket. Brew as you would coffee. Serve hot.

Hot Spice Drink

1 cup brown sugar
1/2 tsp. salt
1 gallon cranberry juice
2 tsp. whole allspice

2 tsp. whole cloves
2 three-inch stick cinnamon
dash nutmeg

Combine brown sugar, salt and cranberry juice. Put in 20-cup or larger coffee percolator. In percolator basket, combine remaining ingredients. Brew as you would coffee. When served, you may add an orange slice floater in each cup, if desired.

Campers' Hot Chocolate Mix

8 qt. pkg. dried milk
2 lb. box Nestle's Quick

6 oz. jar coffee mate powder
1 cup powdered sugar

Mix and keep in container. Put 1/4 cup in each mug. Fill up with hot water or boiling water.

Mocha Mix

2 cups Swiss Miss powder
2 cups powdered non-dairy creamer
1 cup instant coffee granules

1 tsp. cinnamon
1/2 tsp. nutmeg
1 1/4 cups sugar

Blend all ingredients until well mixed. Store in a covered jar. Use 2 tsp. mix per cup of boiling water.

Russian Tea Mix

2 cups Tang
1 1/2 cups sugar
1 tsp. cinnamon

1/2 tsp. cloves
1 cup lemon flavored instant tea

Combine all ingredients and store in covered jar. To serve, mix about 2 tsp. of mixture per cup of hot or ice water.

Swedish Egg Coffee

7 cups water
2 eggs

2/3 cup regular ground coffee
pinch salt

For this, you must use a 10 to 12 cup (minimum) coffee pot, one that sits on the stove, not a perculator. Bring the water to a boil in the coffee pot. Meanwhile, wash the eggs. Combine coffee and salt in a bowl; break the eggs into this mixture. Crush the shells and add them, too. Stir mixture until the ingredients have formed a paste. Stir mixture into the boiling water, watching carefully so it doesn't boil over. Boil gently for 7 minutes. Remove from heat and slowly pour about 1/2 cup cold water over the coffee to settle the grounds. Allow to stand a few minutes, then pour slowly into cups. Makes 8 servings.

GROWING UP

By the time I came along, the house was already full! But, as usual, they made room for one more. It was always that way at our house - very hospitable! My Mom and Dad, Irving and Lois Larson, already had Sharon and Faith in junior high, and Diane and Steve in elementary grades. I stole their hearts anyway, and they babied me a lot (and still do). My Dad was a Baptist pastor, and my Mom kept the household running smoothly, as well as singing in the choir, playing the piano, teaching Sunday School, sewing almost all of our clothes and trying not to get a headache. Then came my baby brother, Jon (now 6'5" tall), only thirteen months after me.

Our house was always full of people; friends of my siblings, folks from my Dad's churches and ten foreign exchange students who lived with us during my school years, along with a few foster kids added in from time to time. Obviously, there was always a lot of activity in the kitchen and plenty of crumbs on the floor for the dog. Thank goodness my parents are both excellent cooks. In fact, my Dad taught my Mom how to cook when they were first married back in 1942.

My parents believed in raising children the old-fashioned way - lots of love for everyone, tough discipline, responsibilities for all and a home centered around Christ.

We all pitched in with the cooking, the cleanup and, of course, the eating! We certainly ate well, the good home-cooked Minnesota Scandinavian meals, even lefse and lutefisk - yuk!

Mealtime included not only eating but such things as lots of laughter (always), Mom reading the "good manners" book (sometimes), discussing Diane's wild hair (most of the time), Steve's facial ticks (usually), Jon's distaste for studying (on occasion), and my boyfriend problems (even at age 6).

As you can tell, growing up in our family was really fun! I thank my parents for creating an environment of love, laughter, and closeness which has continued over the years, through good times and bad, and continues to this day, especially when all 23 of us, including spouses and children, get together.

My parents on their Wedding Day and on their 50th Wedding Anniversary.

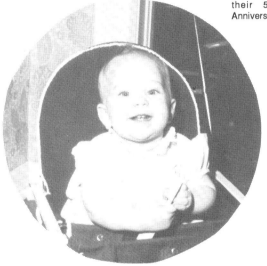

My family's portrait, then . . .

. . . and now.

My brother, Jon, and I are so close in age, everyone thought we were twins.

My brother and I are still best friends.

I've always loved music.

My first formal dress at age 13.

My brother, myself, and three foreign exchange students, waiting for the school bus at the end of the driveway.

Soup &
Sandwiches

Wild Rice Soup

1/2 pound bacon (fried, crumbled, drained)
1 cup wild rice, cooked
1 can cream of potato soup
1 can cream of chicken soup

3 cups milk
1 cup shredded American cheese
dab of minced onion
dab of parsley

Mix ingredients together; add bacon last. Stir and simmer for 10 minutes.

Friendship Cup

1 can tomato soup
1 can beef broth
1 can water

1/4 tsp. marjoram
1/4 tsp. thyme

Combine all ingredients. Simmer 2 minutes, dot with butter.

Cream of Broccoli Soup

1 1/2 lb. broccoli, cut up
2 cups water
3/4 cup chopped celery
1/2 cup chopped onion
2 Tbsp. margarine
1/2 cup whipping cream (or half & half)

dash ground nutmeg
2 Tbsp. flour
2 1/2 cups water
1 1/2 Tbsp. instant chicken bouillon
3/4 tsp. salt
1/8 tsp. pepper

Heat 2 cups water to boiling in 3-quart saucepan. Add broccoli, celery, onion. Cover and heat to boiling. Cook until tender, about 10 minutes; do not drain. Place mixture in blender container and blend until uniform consistency. Heat margarine in 3-quart saucepan over low heat until melted. Stir in flour. Cook, stirring constantly, until mixture is smooth and bubbly; remove from heat. Stir in 2 1/2 cups water. Heat to boiling, stirring constantly. Boil and stir 1 minute. Stir in broccoli mixture, bouillon, salt, pepper, and nutmeg. Heat just to boiling. Stir in cream; heat but do not boil. Serve with grated cheese. Serves 8.

Creamy Broccoli Soup

1/4 cup chopped onion
1 Tbsp. margarine or butter
2 cups milk
8 oz. cream cheese, cubed
dash of pepper

3/4 lb. Velveeta processed cheese
   spread, cubed
10 oz. frozen broccoli, chopped and drained
1/4 tsp. ground nutmeg

In a 3-qt. T-FAL saucepan, saute onions in margarine until tender. Add milk and cream cheese; stir over medium heat until cream cheese is melted. Add remaining ingredients; heat thoroughly, until all cheese is melted, stirring occasionally. Add additional milk if soup is too thick. Makes five 1-cup servings.

Salmon and White Corn Chowder

1/4 lb. bacon
1/2 cup minced onion
2 cups diced potato
1/2 cup chopped celery
1/2 cup chopped carrots
2 cups milk
1 cup water

1 cup chicken broth
1/4 cup white wine
1 can white corn
1 can salmon
dash of salt
dash of white pepper

Saute bacon until crisp in T-FAL 3-quart sauce pan. Reserve drippings. Add onion; saute until softened. Add celery and carrots; saute 5 minutes to soften. Add potatoes and water; simmer for 10-15 minutes or until softened. Add milk, chicken broth and wine; heat through. Add salmon and corn. Salt and pepper to taste. Serve immediately, garnished with whole baby corn on top of each bowl of soup.

Easy Clam Chowder

1 onion, chopped
2 cans clam chowder soup (no tomatoes)
1 can potato soup
milk

2 cans clams
1 can creamed corn
2 Tbsp. butter

Saute onion in butter. Add soups (either concentrate or chunky kind), clams, and creamed corn. Rinse the clam cans out with a little water and put into soup. Add milk until of the consistency you want for soup. Heat through.

French Onion Soup

2 large onions
1 Tbsp. butter
1 tsp. cornstarch
2 (10 1/2 oz. each) cans beef consomme
1 Tbsp. cognac (optional)
salt, if needed

1/2 cup light cream
1 egg yolk, beaten
Worcestershire sauce
Swiss cheese slices, about 12
French bread, toasted

Peel and slice onions into rings. Saute onions in butter until soft and golden. Stir in cornstarch. Add beef consomme, diluted as directed on the can. Simmer about 10 minutes. Add cognac and simmer a little longer. (optional) Add cream and beaten egg yolk, stirring constantly. Add several shakes of worcestershire sauce. Put a piece of cheese on bottom of serving bowl; ladle soup on top. Top with a piece of bread and a piece of cheese. Brown under broiler. About six servings.

Irish Onion Soup

4 large onions
1 1/2 Tbsp. butter
1 1/2 Tbsp. flour
2 cups boiling milk
1 bay leaf
2 cups chicken stock

1/2 tsp. powdered mace or sage
salt
pepper
2 egg yolks
1/2 cup evaporated milk or cream

Mix thinly sliced onions in butter; saute until translucent. Shake flour onto onions. Stir well to absorb butter. Add boiling milk and bay leaf. Continue to stir. Add chicken stock and seasonings. Simmer until onions are cooked. In separate bowl, beat egg yolks and evaporated milk together. Put in bottom of soup tureen and gradually add soup and stir.

Wanton Soup

1/2 lb. ground pork
1 egg
1 Tbsp. grated onion
4 tsp. salt

2 Tbsp. soy sauce
wanton skins
6 cups chicken broth

Brown ground pork. Combine with egg, onion, 2 tsp. salt and 1 Tbsp. soy sauce. Wrap small amount of meat mixture in wanton skin, fold in triangle and wet edges with water to stick together. Combine chicken stock, 1 Tbsp. soy sauce and 2 tsp. salt. Add filled wantons and simmer until heated through.

Mom's Cheese Soup

1 onion, chopped
1/4 cup butter
1/2 cup flour
salt and pepper to taste
2 cups milk
1 tsp. mustard

1 can chicken broth (10-12 oz.)
8 oz. jar Cheese Whiz or 1 lb. Velveeta
a little water
vegetables, already cooked (may be frozen),
    any variety such as carrots, broccoli,
    peas, beans, mixed, etc.

Fry chopped onion in butter. Add flour, salt and pepper to taste. Then add milk and bring to a boil; boil 1 minute. Add chicken broth, cheese, a little water, vegetables and mustard. Heat through and serve.

Swedish Fruit Soup

3/4 cup prunes
5 cups water
1/4 cup large tapioca
1 stick cinnamon
3/4 cup raisins
1/4 orange, sliced very thin

juice of remaining orange
peel of 1/2 lemon, grated
juice of 1/2 lemon
1/2 cup sugar
3/4 tsp. salt
2 cups cooked apples (or 1 can pie apples)

Combine prunes, water and tapioca in large kettle; simmer 45 minutes. Using a smaller kettle, boil the cinnamon stick, raisins, orange, orange juice, lemon juice and rind until orange slices are tender. Add sugar and salt; combine with prunes. Add cooked apples. Note: Do not cook after apples are added. Serve hot or cold. Makes about 1 1/2 quarts.

Cream of Potato Soup

6 cups frozen hash brown potatoes
1/2 cup sliced carrots
6 slices bacon
1 cup chopped celery
1 chopped onion
finely shredded cheddar cheese

1 1/2 tsp. salt
1 tsp. pepper
2 cups milk
2 cups light cream or half-and-half
parsley sprigs

Cook potatoes and carrots in water until tender. Drain. Saute bacon until crisp; drain and crumble. Saute onion and celery in 2 Tbsp. bacon fat. Combine all remaining ingredients, except shredded cheese and parsley, and simmer for 30 minutes. Don't boil. Garnish with the shredded cheese and parsley. Makes 2 quarts. Note: If desired, you may combine all ingredients in your crock pot without any pre-cooking and cook on low all day. You will still want to do bacon separately or you may use bacon bits for the crunchy taste.

Potato Soup

6 potatoes, cubed
2 carrots, sliced
2 celery stems, sliced
2 onions, diced
1 Tbsp. parsley, chopped

salt & pepper to taste
5 cups water
4 chicken bouillon cubes
13 oz. evaporated milk
1/3 cup margarine

Combine all ingredients except milk and margarine. Cook over medium heat for 40 minutes, covered. Add milk and margarine and simmer for 30 more minutes on low.

Diet Soup

1 large onion
4 ribs celery
46 oz. tomato juice
2 to 3 cups water
a shake of pepper
1 small pinch sweet basil
3 sprinkles seasoned salt

4 carrots
1/2 head cabbage, shredded
6 beef bouillon cubes
1 big pinch dried parsley
3 sprinkles thyme
2 sprinkles garlic salt
1 bay leaf

Chop vegetables. Combine all ingredients in large kettle and cover and simmer at least 1 hour. Remove bay leaf before serving. Makes about 3 quarts of soup, about 30 calories per cup.

English Beef Soup

10 cups beef stock
 8 oz. or more beef chuck roast
1 tsp. Worcestershire sauce
1/2 tsp. basil
1 tsp. chopped chives
2 bay leaves
1 tsp. salt
dash pepper

1/2 cup tomatoes
1/4 cup barley
3 large carrots, chopped
2 cups celery, chopped
3 medium onions, chopped
2 Tbsp. margarine
1 Tbsp. flour

Defat and cube beef roast; brown in a little oil. Add to beef stock. Add remaining ingredients, except margarine and flour, and cook until barley and vegetables are tender. In a small saucepan, melt butter; add flour and cook, stirring constantly, for a couple minutes, but do not brown. Add some soup broth to flour mixture to make a paste. Add paste to soup, just enough to slightly thicken the soup.

Cheeseburger Soup

1/2 cup shredded carrots	1 lb. Velveeta cheese
1/3 cup chopped celery	1 can cheddar cheese soup
1/4 cup chopped onion	2 soup cans of milk
3 cups chicken broth	8 oz. sour cream
2 cups cooked rice	chives
1 lb. cooked hamburger	

Simmer the first four ingredients for 10 minutes. Add the remaining ingredients, except sour cream and chives, and cook until cheese is melted. Do not boil. Add sour cream and chives just before serving.

Hamburger Vegetable Soup

1 lb. hamburger	1/4 tsp. thyme
1 cup chopped onion	1/4 cup rice
1 cup diced, cooked potatoes	3 cups water
1 cup sliced carrots	2 tsp. salt
1 cup shredded cabbage	1/4 tsp. basil
1 cup sliced celery	1 bay leaf
2 cups tomatoes	

Brown hamburger and onion. Add remaining ingredients and simmer at least one hour. 220 calories per cup

Vegetable Meat Ball Soup

1/2 lb. ground beef	1/2 tsp. salt
1 cup softened bread crumbs	dash oregano
dash pepper	1 Tbsp. margarine or butter
dash garlic powder	3 cups water
1 pkg. Lipton Country Vegetable soup mix	1 can whole tomatoes, chopped
1 egg	1 beef bouillon cube

In small bowl, combine egg, ground beef, bread crumbs, pepper, salt, oregano and garlic powder; blend well. Shape into about 20 marble-size meatballs. In medium skillet, melt butter and cook meat balls until lightly browned. Drain off excess fat. Add soup mix to meat balls in skillet. Blend in water, tomatoes and beef bouillon cube. Bring to a boil, stirring occasionally. Partially cover and simmer 15 minutes. Serves 2.

Sloppy Joes

3 lbs. ground beef
1 cup ketchup
1/2 cup brown sugar
dash of lemon juice

1 tsp. garlic powder
1 can chicken gumbo soup
salt & pepper to taste

Brown ground beef, adding garlic powder, salt and pepper to taste. Add ketchup, brown sugar, lemon and soup. Heat and serve on hamburger buns. Makes 2 dozen sloppy joes.

Barbeque Beef Sandwiches

2 lb. beef roast
2 Tbsp. margarine
1/4 cup minced onions
1/4 cup white vinegar

1/3 cup brown sugar
2 tsp. dry mustard
2 Tbsp. Worcestershire sauce
1 cup ketchup

Bake roast until tender. Pull into strips. Blend remaining ingredients and mix with beef.

Pizza Cups

3/4 lb. ground beef
salt, pepper and garlic salt to taste
1/2 cup ketchup or barbeque sauce
2 Tbsp. brown sugar

1 Tbsp. minced onion
3/4 cup grated cheddar cheese
8 oz. can refrigerator biscuits

Brown meat; season with salt, pepper and a little garlic salt. Drain fat. Add ketchup or barbeque sauce, onion and brown sugar. Roll out dough. Place rolled dough into greased muffin cups, making sure dough goes up the sides. Fill with cooked meat mixture and top with cheese. Bake in 400 degree oven for 10-12 minutes.

Diane's Pizza Burgers

1 lb. ground beef
2 tsp. oregano
8 oz. mozzarella cheese

2 cups canned spaghetti sauce
1/2 tsp. salt
1 tsp. sage

Brown ground beef. Cool. Add seasonings and spaghetti sauce. Put on bun half. Top with thin slice of cheese. Bake 12 minutes at 425 degrees.

Faith's Pizza Burgers

1 lb. hamburger
1/4 cup ketchup
3 Tbsp. chili sauce
2 Tbsp. mustard

1 tsp. worcestershire sauce
2 Tbsp. minced onion
1/2 tsp. salt
dash pepper

Combine all ingredients. Put on hamburger bun halves; top with cheese, if desired (slices or grated). Bake at 425 degrees for 12 minutes or broil for 5 minutes. Makes 20 pizza burger halves.

Hot Tuna Buns

1 can tuna fish
3 hard-boiled eggs, diced
2 Tbsp. onion, finely chopped
2 Tbsp. sweet pickles, finely chopped

1 lb. American cheese, grated
2 Tbsp. green pepper, finely chopped
2 Tbsp. stuffed olives, finely chopped
1/2 cup mayonnaise

Mix all ingredients and spread between hamburger buns (1 1/2 to 2 dozen.) Place the buns in a covered roaster or cake pan covered with foil and bake for 30 minutes at 350 degrees.

Tuna Burgers

1 can tuna (or 1 cup chicken)
1/3 cup mayonnaise
chopped onion, as desired
chopped green pepper, as desired

2 hard boiled eggs, chopped
1/2 cup sour cream
parmesan cheese

Mix together. Spread on halves of hamburger buns. Sprinkle with parmesan cheese. Broil until bubbly. Serves about 8.

French-Toasted Ham and Cheese

1 loaf Italian bread
8 oz. pkg. ham slices
8 oz. mozzarella cheese slices
1/4 cup milk

2 eggs
1/4 cup butter or margarine
1 cup maple syrup

Cut 12 slices from Italian bread, each about 1/2-inch thick. Fold ham and cheese slices to fit on 6 bread slices; top with remaining bread slices to make 6 sandwiches. In pie plate, beat milk and eggs with fork until well mixed. Dip sandwiches into egg mixture, one at a time, until well coated on both sides. In 12-inch skillet (T-Fal works great) over medium-low heat, in hot butter or margarine, cook sandwiches until golden brown on both sides, about 15 minutes. Meanwhile, in a small saucepan over low heat, heat maple syrup until hot but not boiling. Serve sandwiches with maple syrup.

Hot Deviled Ham Sandwiches

1 onion, chopped
1 green pepper, chopped
1 lb. shredded sharp cheddar cheese
1/4 cup ketchup
6 Tbsp. sweet pickle relish

5 oz. deviled ham
1/2 cup cream
1/4 cup melted butter
hamburger buns

Mix all ingredients together and put on hamburger buns. Wrap filled buns in foil and bake 10 minutes at 400 degrees.

Super Sandwich

3/4 lb. American cheese
1/2 lb. Spam
1 medium onion, chopped

1 small jar stuffed olives
1 small can tomato paste
hotdog buns

Put cheese, Spam, onion and olives in food grinder. Add tomato paste. Put in hotdog buns, wrap in foil, and bake 30 minutes at 350 degrees.

Crescent Chicken Rolls

3 oz. cream cheese
2 Tbsp. margarine
2 cups cooked and cubed chicken
1/4 tsp. salt
1/8 tsp. pepper

2 Tbsp. milk
1 Tbsp. chopped green onion
1 Tbsp. chopped pimento
8 oz. can crescent rolls
Italian bread crumbs

Blend cream cheese and 2 Tbsp. margarine. Add chicken, salt, pepper, milk, green onion and pimento. Mix well. Separate crescent rolls into 4 rectangles, sealing the perforations. Spoon chicken mixture into center of each rectangle. Pull edges (corners) together and seal all edges. Brush with melted butter and dip or sprinkle bread crumbs on top. Bake at 350 degrees on ungreased cookie sheet for 20-25 minutes or until deep golden brown. Makes 4 lunch or dinner-sized rolls.

Chicken Salad Sandwiches

1 chicken, cooked, deboned and
    cut up in small pieces
1 cup finely chopped celery

1/4 cup finely chopped onion
2 1/4 cups Miracle Whip Salad Dressing

Mix all ingredients and chill for several hours before serving. Put on bread, rolls or croissants. Will fill 36 petite croissants or 12 large croissants.

HIGH SCHOOL

I didn't date much and I wasn't voted Homecoming Queen, but I was involved in just about everything else while in high school.

I loved being a cheerleader for both basketball and football for all four years, jumping up and down, doing the splits, hooting and hollering for our team and wondering if any of the jocks would ever ask me out.

I also loved to sing! I was in the school choir and competed at a lot of music contests. I also sang in two different high school singing groups from my church that toured around the Midwest, ministering at various churches.

The true highlight of these years was being in our champion high school band. To this day, the Long Prairie High School Band is rated as one of the top bands in the country. I was one of the head majorettes and a field commander who directed the music on a podium during a field show on the football field. This was a great experience in self-discipline and teamwork, which earned us first place trophies at every parade for a period of about four to five years. This gave us the opportunity to travel to several locations, such as Florida, Washington, D.C., Alberta, Canada, and most memorable to me, the Tournament of Roses parade in Pasadena, during the Bicentennial year of 1976! What a gorgeous parade route that was, but seven miles long! My feet ached for days from those high-heeled, knee-high, white go-go boots!

Needless to say, I wasn't around much to help Mom with the dishes, but my parents always made sure I found time for studying and a little part-time secretarial work during the summer to earn money for college.

All in all, these are the things memories are made of and I'm glad I was able to experience so many things, some of which are still very much a part of my life.

My Graduation Photos   Yea, Team!!

Flipper

FLIPPER, the friendly dolphin, came out of the water to say "hi" to Mary Beth Larson (left), Judy Zeller, and Cathy Steinert; the Aquatennial Queen.

Flipper had just finished a performance at Marineland and the Marching M'Bassadors were to perform next.

I was head majorette (far left, above) when our band went to the Tournament of Roses Parade in Pasadena. We visited Marineland and this article appeared in the newspaper.

Salads

Pistachio Salad

3 1/2 oz. box instant pistachio pudding
1 large can (16-20 oz.) crushed pineapple
8 oz. Cool Whip

1/2 bag mini marshmallows
chopped nuts
maraschino cherries

Blend dry pudding mix and Cool Whip; add pineapple and marshamallows. Top with nuts and cherries.

Tapioca Salad

1 pkg. vanilla tapioca pudding
1 pkg. orange tapioca pudding
1 can pineapple tidbits

1 can mandarin oranges
1 1/2 cups miniature marshmallows
8 oz. Cool Whip

Drain the fruit; reserve liquid. Add water to fruit liquid to make 3 cups. Use this liquid to cook the puddings until thick. Cool thoroughly. Add the pineapple and oranges and miniature marshmallows. Fold in Cool Whip and refrigerate.

Overnight Salad

21 oz. can lemon pie filling
1 cup whipping cream, whipped
1 large can fruit cocktail, drained

1 can pineapple tidbits, drained
1 can mandarin oranges, drained
1 1/2 cups miniature marshmallows

Combine all ingredients and let stand overnight in refrigerator. Keeps well.

Cranberry Christmas Salad

13 1/2 oz. can crushed pineapple
6 oz. pkg. strawberry jello
3/4 cup cold water
16 oz. can jellied cranberry sauce
1/3 cup chopped pecans

1 Tbsp. butter or margarine
1 small pkg. vanilla instant pudding mix
1/2 cup whipping cream
1/2 cup milk
3 oz. cream cheese, softened

Drain pineapple juice into a measuring cup; reserve pineapple. Add water to juice to make 1 cup liquid. Bring liquid to a boil in a saucepan over medium heat. When boiling, remove from heat, stir in jellopowder and stir until jello is dissolved. Add cold water; chill until jello is of the consistency of unbeaten egg whites. In medium-size bowl, combine drained pineapple and cranberry sauce; when well mixed, stir into jello mixture. Pour into a 9-inch square cake pan. Cover and chill until firm. Meanwhile, heat oven to 350 degrees. Place pecans and butter in shallow pan and bake about 8 minutes, stirring occasionally, until pecans are toasted. Cool pecans. When jello mixture is firm, combine pudding mix, whipping cream and milk in a bowl. Beat until well blended, about 1 minute. Add cream cheese and blend well. Spread over the jello. Sprinkle pecans over frosting. Chill 2 to 3 hours, until frosting is firm.

Cranberry Relish

1 pkg. cranberries
1 orange
1 cup sugar
1 small can crushed pineapple (optional)

6 oz. pkg. raspberry jello
1 cup chopped celery
1 cup chopped nuts

Grind 1 orange with rind and cranberries. Cover with sugar; stir and let set 1 hour. Mix jello powder with cranberry mixture. Add drained pineapple, chopped celery and nuts. Will keep in the refrigerator for 1 to 2 weeks.

Cranberry Salad

1 lb. (2 cups) cranberries
1 cup sugar
1 can crushed pineapple

1 cup walnuts, chopped
3 cups miniature marshmallows
8 oz. Cool Whip

Grind cranberries. Add remaining ingredients and mix well. Chill.

Party-Size Fruit Salad

1 pkg. (7 oz.) ring macaroni
1 can (13 1/2 oz.) crushed pineapple
1 unpeeled apple, diced
1 banana, diced
1 pint strawberries, sliced

1 pint whipping cream
4 eggs
1 cup sugar
1/3 cup lemon juice
2 Tbsp. flour

Cook macaroni as directed on package; drain. Drain pineapple, reserving juice for dressing. Add pineapple to macaroni. In saucepan, beat 4 eggs slightly. Add reserved pineapple juice, sugar, lemon juice and flour. Cook until thickened over low heat, stirring constantly. Pour hot dressing over macaroni and pineapple. Fold in diced apples, banana, and strawberries. Refrigerate for several hours or overnight. Shortly before serving, whip cream until it forms soft peaks; blend into salad. Serves 18 to 20.

Frozen Mini Fruit Salads

16 oz. sour cream
2/3 cup sugar
1 1/2 Tbsp. lemon juice
pinch salt
1 medium banana, mashed

8 1/4 oz. can crushed pineapple, drained
1/3 cup chopped pecans
1/3 cup maraschino cherries, drained and
    quartered
2 1/2 Tbsp. maraschino cherry juice

Line muffin cups with paper baking cups. In large bowl, combine sour cream, sugar, lemon juice and salt; mix well. Stir in remaining ingredients. Fill muffin cups 3/4 full. Freeze. Let stand at room temperature 5 minutes before serving. Makes 10-12 salads.

Ambrosia Salad for 50

12 lbs. fruit, fresh or canned
    (bananas, oranges, grapes, apples)
1 dozen eggs
juice of 4 lemons
coconut

2 qt. or 4 lbs. pineapple chunks
1 qt. pineapple juice
    (saved from draining pineapple chunks)
2 cups sugar
2 qt. heavy cream

Prepare fruit in bite size pieces. Drain pineapple, saving juice, and combine with other fruit, then set fruit aside. Beat eggs until thick, then beat in pineapple juice, lemon juice, and sugar. Cook this mixture over boiling water until thick and then let it cool. Whip cream and fold into cooled egg mixture. Mix in fruit and chill. Serve on a lettuce leaf and sprinkle coconut on top.

Lush Mush

1 Tbsp. (1 envelope) unflavored gelatin
2 Tbsp. cold water
1 1/2 cups orange juice
12 large marshmallows

1/2 cup lemon juice
2 cups heavy cream
1 No. 2 can fruit cocktail, drained

Soften gelatin in cold water. Heat 1/2 cup orange juice and marshmallows in top of double boiler over hot water until marshmallows are melted. Add softened gelatin. Stir until dissolved. Add remaining orange and lemon juice. Cool. Whip cream and add gelatin mixture gradually. Partially fill bottom of sherbet glasses with fruit cocktail. Pour gelatin mixture over fruit. Chill. Top with maraschino cherry. Serves 6 or 8.

Black Walnut Salad

1 pkg. lemon jello
1 cup crushed pineapple
9 large marshmallows
8 oz. cream cheese

1 cup water plus pineapple juice from
   crushed pineapple
chopped walnuts
1 cup Cool Whip

Heat jello and water in saucepan; add marshmallows and cheese, stirring until all melted. Let sit until cooled a little. Add remaining ingredients. Put in mold or bowl and chill to set.

Pink Delight Salad

8 oz. cream cheese
8 oz. marachino cherries,
   cut up (save juice)

1 No. 2 can crushed pineapple, drained
8 to 10 oz. miniature marshmallows
1 pint whipping cream, whipped

Cream cheese with cherry juice; mix well. Add rest of ingredients and fold in whipped cream. Refrigerate a few hours before serving.

Pink Salad

8 oz. cream cheese, softened
2-3 oz. pkgs. strawberry jello
2/3 cup sugar
2 cups hot water

1 cup chopped nuts
16 oz. crushed pineapple, drained
16 oz. Cool Whip

Dissolve jello in hot water with sugar. Add cream cheese; stir until blended. Chill until partly set. Add nuts, pineapple and Cool Whip and beat with hand beater. Pour into mold or dish and chill.

Cherry Coke Salad

1 cup canned pitted cherries, drained
3/4 cup sugar
1/2 cup water
6 oz. cherry jello mix

1 cup nuts, optional
1 cup crushed pineapple, drained
1 (12 oz.) Coke

Combine cherries, sugar and water; bring to boil and boil one minute. Add jello powder, nuts and pineapple. Mix together; then add Coke. Chill and serve.

Pear Velvet Salad

16 oz. can pears
3 oz. pkg. lime jello

8 oz. cream cheese
8 oz. Cool Whip

Strain pears and bring juice to boil. Dissolve jello in pear juice. Combine pears, cheese and 4 Tbsp. jello mixture in blender and blend until smooth. Add remaining jello mixture and blend again. Refrigerate until soft-set and fold in Cool Whip. Chill several hours.

Blueberry Salad

1 can blueberry pie filling
6 oz. pkg. raspberry jello
1/2 cup chopped nuts

8 oz. Cool Whip
1 or 2 bananas

Prepare jello as directed on package. Put in refrigerator until almost jelled. Stir in blueberry pie filling. Chill until set. Slice bananas and put on jello, then sprinkle nuts over bananas and add Cool Whip on top. Easy and good!

Peach Salad

1 can mandarin oranges, drained
1 can peach pie filling

1 can pineapple tidbits, drained
2 bananas

Mix all together. Serve on a lettuce leaf as a salad or plain as a dessert.

Apple Fluff

3 oz. pkg. jello, any flavor
1 cup boiling water
2/3 cup cold water
1 1/2 cups applesauce

1 tsp. grated lemon rind
1/4 tsp. cinnamon
1/8 tsp. cloves

Dissolve jello in boiling water. Stir in cold water. Chill about one hour or until it begins to thicken; then beat until light and fluffy and double in volume. Fold in applesauce, lemon rind, cinnamon and cloves. Spoon mixture into 8x8" pan. Chill until set. Serve topped with whipped cream or on lettuce. Serves 6-8.

Lime Salad

3/4 cup cold water
2 oz. cream cheese
3 oz. box lime jello
15 large marshmallows
1 cup diced bananas

1 tsp. lemon juice
1 small can crushed pineapple
1/2 cup mayonnaise
1/2 cup milk
1/2 cup chopped nuts

Combine cold water, cream cheese, lime jello powder and marshmallows. Stir over low heat until melted. Stir in remaining ingredients. Chill.

Mandarin Orange Salad

2 cups boiling water
6 oz. pkg. orange jello
6 oz. can frozen orange juice, undiluted
2 cans mandarin oranges

1 can crushed pineapple
1 pkg. instant lemon pudding
1 cup milk
1/2 pint whipping cream, whipped

Mix boiling water with jello until dissolved. Add frozen orange juice, mandarin oranges and crushed pineapple. Chill until firm. Mix instant lemon pudding and milk as directed on box; fold in whipped cream. Spread over jello.

Coconut Orange Salad

16 oz. sour cream
15 oz. mandarin oranges, drained

10 oz. miniature marshmallows
2 cups flake coconut

Mix sour cream and miniature marshmallows. Fold in oranges and coconut. Easy to fix and ready to serve!

Orange Jello

6 oz. pkg. orange jello
2 cups boiling water

1 pint orange sherbet
1 can mandarin oranges, drained

Dissolve jello in boiling water. Add sherbet; stir until melted. Add mandarin oranges. Chill in refrigerator until set.

Spring Salad

3 oz. pkg. orange jello
1/4 cup sugar
1 1/2 cups boiling water
8 oz. cream cheese, softened

1/2 cup orange juice
2 Tbsp. lemon juice
1 cup shredded carrots
1 cup finely chopped celery

Dissolve jello and sugar in boiling water. Add orange juice and cream cheese; stir until blended. Add remaining ingredients. Pour into serving dish; refrigerate until firm.

Yummy Raspberry Salad

6 oz. pkg. raspberry jello
3 oz. pkg. vanilla pudding mix
3 1/2 cups water

16 oz. sweetened raspberries, fresh or
    frozen
8 oz. Cool Whip

Mix jello powder and pudding mix in pan; stir in 3 1/2 cups water slowly. Cook to boil, stirring constantly; boil for 2 minutes.   Refrigerate until slightly jelled. Fold in raspberries and Cool Whip. Chill until set.

Do-Ahead Pineapple Salad

3 Tbsp + 1/2 cup sugar
1 Tbsp. cornstarch
pinch of salt
2 egg yolks
1 cup pineapple juice

1 cup whipping cream
1 tsp. vanilla
10 oz. miniature marshmallows
1 can crushed pineapple, drained
2 Tbsp. lemon juice

Combine 3 Tbsp. sugar, cornstarch, salt, egg yolks and pineapple juice; beat well and cook in top of double boiler until thick. Cool. Whip the whipping cream; add 1/2 cup sugar and vanilla. Fold into cooled custard with marshmallows, crushed pineapple (drained), and lemon juice. Chill for at least 24 hours. Serves 8.

Pineapple-Strawberry Salad

6 oz. pkg. strawberry jello
16 oz. frozen strawberries
1 small can crushed pineapple, well-drained
2 bananas, mashed

1/2 pint whipping cream
8 oz. cream cheese, softened
1 cup powdered sugar
1 tsp. vanilla

Dissolve jello in 2 cups boiling water; reserve 1/4 cup of mixture. Add berries, stirring until thawed. Add pineapple and bananas; pour into a 9-inch square pan and chill until set. Whip cream until stiff. Blend the cream cheese, sugar, reserved gelatin mixture, and vanilla. Fold in whipped cream. Spread this mixture over jello. Sprinkle with chopped nuts and chill until set. Cut into squares. Serves 9.

Quick Strawberry Salad

16 oz. Cool Whip
6 oz. box strawberry jello
22 oz. small curd cottage cheese

strawberries, 1 cup fresh, sliced or
    10 oz. frozen, thawed and drained
1/2 cup chopped nuts (optional)

Mix together the jello powder and cottage cheese. Fold in Cool Whip. Add fruit and nuts. Ready to serve immediately or may be stored in refrigerator. This is delicious and no one will guess there's cottage cheese in it!

Strawberry Salad

1/3 cup butter
1 1/2 cups crushed vanilla wafers
3 oz. pkg. strawberry jello
3/4 cup boiling water
1 can sweetened condensed milk

10 oz. frozen, sliced strawberries,
*   in syrup, thawed*
4 cups miniature marshmallows
1 cup whipping cream, whipped

In saucepan, melt butter; stir in crumbs. Pat into 11x7 pan; chill. Dissolve jello in boiling water. Stir in milk and undrained strawberries. Fold in marshmallows and whipped cream. Pour on crumbs. Chill.

Strawberry Sour Cream Salad

6 oz. pkg strawberry jello
2 cups boiling water
1 or 2 pkg. frozen strawberries

1 can crushed pineapple
2 bananas, sliced
1 cup sour cream

Dissolve jello in water; add strawberries, bananas and pineapple. Pour half of mixture into 9x13 pan. Chill until firm. Spoon sour cream over top, spread evenly and cover with remaining jello mixture. Chill and serve.

Berry Velvet Cream

3 oz. pkg. strawberry or raspberry jello
1 cup whipping cream, whipped

10 oz. strawberries or raspberries
*   (if frozen, thawed and drained)*

Dissolve jello as directed on package, using 1 cup boiling water and berry juice with cold water to make 1 cup. Chill until almost firm. Beat gelatin until foamy. Fold together whipped jello, whipped cream and drained berries. Spoon into 1-qt. mold or 6 to 8 individual molds. Chill until firm.

Strawberry Pretzel Salad

2 cups pretzels, crushed
3 Tbsp.+ 1/2 cup sugar
3/4 cup margarine, melted
8 oz. cream cheese

8 oz. Cool Whip
6 oz. pkg. strawberry gelatin
2 cups boiling water
20 oz. frozen strawberries

Mix pretzels, 3 Tbsp. sugar and melted margarine. Put into a 9x13-inch pan. Bake at 350 degrees for 10 minutes. Let cool. Cream softened cream cheese. Beat in 1/2 cup sugar; fold in Cool Whip. Put over cooled crust. Chill. Dissolve gelatin in boiling water, add thawed strawberries and pour on top of cheese layer. Chill; cut in squares when firm.

Ginger Ale Salad

3 oz. pkg. jello, any flavor
1/2 cup boiling water
1 1/2 cups ginger ale

2 Tbsp. lemon juice
4 Tbsp. sugar
fruit of your choice

Dissolve jello in 1/2 cup boiling water. Add ginger ale, lemon juice and sugar. Stir until sugar is dissolved. Cool. When mixture begins to thicken, fold in fruit of your choice, such as 1 cup sliced canned peaches or pears; mandarin orange sections; fresh strawberries, sliced; seedless grapes, cut in half; or diced canned pineapple. Nice with this salad is a Strawberry Sour Cream Dressing: 2 cups sour cream, 1 tsp. salt and 1/2 cup fresh mashed or frozen strawberries.

Chicken Salad

3 cups diced chicken
2 cups diced celery
1/2 cup mayonnaise or salad dressing
1/4 cup chopped sweet pickles

3 Tbsp. lemon juice
1 tsp. salt
1/4 tsp. pepper

Combine chicken and celery. In a separate bowl, combine all other ingredients. Add chicken and celery. Let chill for one hour.

Chicken Salad Deluxe

1 box macaroni rings, cooked
1 cup diced celery
2 cups cut green grapes
1 cup flaked coconut
1 large can crushed pineapple, drained

1 large can pineapple tidbits, drained
4 cups chicken, cut up
16 oz. Cool Whip
1 to 2 cups real mayonnaise

Cook macaroni according to directions; drain. Add celery, grapes, coconut, pineapple and chicken. Mix together the Cool Whip and mayonnaise. Add to salad and blend well. Refrigerate.

Tuna-Carrot Salad

1 can boned chicken
1 can tuna
1 1/2 tsp. grated onion
2 cups celery, chopped

1 1/2 cups grated carrots
1 cup salad dressing
1 can shoe string potatoes

Mix together everything except shoe string potatoes. Chill for one hour or more. Just before serving, stir in shoe string potatoes. (Chow mein noodles may be substituted for the shoe string potatoes.)

Tuna Macaroni Salad (Large Group)

3 boxes ring macaroni, prepared
10 hardboiled eggs, chopped
2 oz. pimento, chopped
1/3 stalk celery, chopped
4 cans tuna, drained
1 large onion, chopped fine

1 can very young, small peas, drained
1/2 tsp. pepper
2 Tbsp. salt
2 1/2 tsp. seasoned salt
Miracle Whip (or other salad dressing)

Mix together and add Miracle Whip Salad Dressing to desired consistency. Refrigerate. Best if chilled several hours before (or day before) serving. About 40 servings.

Shrimp Salad

1/2 cup raw rice, cooked
4 1/2 oz. can shrimp
1/2 cup green pepper, chopped
1 cup onion, chopped
1 cup small raw cauliflower sections

6 stuffed olives, sliced
juice of 1/2 lemon
1/4 cup mayonnaise
salt, pepper, tabasco to taste

Mix shrimp, rice, vegetables and lemon juice. Add seasonings and mayonnaise. Stir again.
Serve on greens.

Shrimp and Macaroni Salad

1 box (7 oz.) macaroni
2 Tbsp. lemon juice
2 cups Miracle Whip
1 lb. white grapes, cut up
1/4 cup chopped onion

1/4 cup celery, diced
1 small pkg. slivered almonds
2 cups small shrimp, drained
8 oz. Cool Whip

The night before, cook the macaroni; rinse and drain. Marinate overnight in lemon juice
and 1 cup Miracle Whip. Next day, add grapes, onion, celery, almonds, and shrimp. Mix;
add Cool Whip and remaining 1 cup Miracle Whip.

Taco Salad

1 lb. hamburger
1 pkg. taco seasoning
1/2 cup water
1 bottle Kraft Miracle French dressing
1 large head lettuce

3-4 tomatoes, chopped
1/2 lb. grated cheddar cheese
12 oz. pkg. Doritos, crushed
1 can kidney beans, drained & rinsed

Brown hamburger; season with salt and pepper to taste. Chill. Mix taco seasoning packet
with water in small saucepan and simmer for a few minutes. Set aside and cool. Tear up
head of lettuce into bite-sized pieces; add cheese, tomatoes, kidney beans and crushed
Doritos. Mix together the taco seasoning sauce and dressing. Just before serving, pour
dressing mix over salad and stir.

Rainbow Pasta Parmesan

8 oz. cream cheese
3/4 cup milk
1/2 cup grated parmesan cheese
dash of nutmeg

dash of pepper
12 oz. rainbow colored pasta, cooked
2 Tbsp. margarine

Melt cream cheese and milk over low heat in a T-FAL 3-quart sauce pan. Add 1/4 cup parmesan cheese, cooked pasta, margarine and spices. Toss to coat. Serve warm with remaining parmesan cheese sprinkled on top.

Rainbow Pasta Salad

1 lb. rainbow macaroni
1 bottle Italian dressing
1/2 bottle salad supreme seasoning,
    about 4 Tbsp.

a little basil, oregano and garlic powder
any raw vegetables, any amount, such
    as tomato, onion, pepper, broccoli,
    cauliflower

Prepare macaroni according to directions on box. Drain and cool. Add remaining ingredients.

Macaroni Salad for a Crowd

6 lbs. macaroni, cooked and drained
5 dozen hard boiled eggs, chopped or
    sliced
1 bunch celery, chopped
3 large onions, chopped
4 cups radishes, sliced
6 large cucumbers, peeled and chopped

1 Tbsp. celery salt
1 quart mayonnaise or salad dressing
1 cup milk
1/2 cup vinegar mixed with
    2 Tbsp. sugar
1/4 cup prepared mustard

Combine salad dressing, milk, vinegar mixed with sugar and mustard. Pour over macaroni and other ingredients mixed together. Best when made several hours ahead or the day before. Serves about 100 people.

Harvest Coleslaw

4 cups cabbage, shredded
1 cup diced tomatoes
1/2 cup chopped celery
1/4 cup chopped onion
1/4 lb. cheese, cubed or shredded

1 cup Miracle Whip
1/4 cup french dressing
1/8 cup sugar
1 tsp. salt
dash pepper

Combine cabbage, tomatoes, celery, onion, and cheese. Mix together remaining dressing ingredients and mix with salad. Refrigerate.

Creamy Cole Slaw

1 cup mayonnaise
1/4 cup milk
2 Tbsp. sugar
1 tsp. salt

1/2 onion, finely chopped
1 head cabbage, shredded
1-2 carrots, shredded
1 green pepper, finely chopped

Mix mayonnaise, milk, sugar and salt. Add remaining ingredients and blend well.

Oriental Salad

1 large head Napa Chinese cabbage
5-7 green onions and tops
3 pkg. Ramen noodles (omit flavor packets)
1/2 cup salted sunflower seeds
1 pkg. slivered almonds
2 Tbsp. sesame seeds

1/2 cup butter
1/2 cup vegetable oil
1/2 cup red cider vinegar
1/2 cup sugar
2 Tbsp. soy sauce

Chop cabbage and green onions and tops. Combine in large bowl and set aside. Break up Ramen noodles and combine in frying pan with sunflower seeds, almonds, sesame seeds and butter. Brown; drain on paper towels. Combine oil, vinegar, sugar and soy sauce in saucepan. Bring to a boil; boil 1 minute, then cool. Combine all ingredients in large bowl and serve.

Lettuce Layer Salad

1 head lettuce
minced onion
Salad Supreme
16 oz. frozen peas
8 oz. grated American or Cheddar cheese

2 cups Miracle Whip
sugar
1 jar Bacos or 1 lb. bacon, fried and
    crumbled

Break lettuce into bite size pieces in rectangular glass dish. Sprinkle onion and Salad Supreme on lettuce. Spread peas over lettuce. Spread Miracle Whip on top to cover entire salad. (Use more Miracle Whip if necessary). Sprinkle sugar over all of the Miracle Whip. Layer cheese and bacon on top. Refrigerate overnight.

Raspberry-Rice Salad

1 cup rice
3 cups milk
1 cup sugar

2 cups whipping cream, whipped
20 oz. frozen raspberries
2 Tbsp. cornstarch

Add milk and sugar to rice. Cook slowly for approximately 25 minutes until milk is gone. Cool. Stir in whipped cream. Drain raspberries, reserving juice. Add cornstarch to juice; heat until smooth. Add raspberries and cook an additional 3 minutes. Cool and top over rice.

Easy Potato Salad

1/2 cup mayonnaise
1/2 cup sour cream
1/2 tsp. salt
1/2 tsp. mustard
1/2 cup onion, finely chopped

dash of pepper
4 large potatoes, boiled and cubed
2-3 hard boiled eggs, chopped
1 cup celery

Mix together mayonnaise, sour cream, salt, mustard, onion and pepper. Stir in potatoes, eggs and celery. Chill at least one hour (even overnight) before serving.

Potato Salad for 50 people

10 lbs. potatoes, cooked and diced
2 dozen eggs, hard-boiled and chopped
1 medium bunch celery, chopped
1 lb. carrots, grated
2-3 onions, diced
1 quart salad dressing (Miracle Whip)

1 pint whipping cream, whipped
1 pint half-and-half
4 1/2 oz. prepared mustard
3/4 cup sugar (optional)
3 1/2 tsp. salt
1/2 tsp. coarse pepper

Combine cooked, diced potatoes, chopped eggs, celery, carrots, and onions. Sprinkle with salt and pepper. Mix together salad dressing, whipped cream, half-and-half, and mustard (for a sweeter dressing, add sugar). Pour over salad and blend. Best when made the day before and allowed to refrigerate overnight. If desired, sprinkle with paprika and garnish with thin sliced eggs and radishes.

Veggie/Fruit Salad

1 bunch broccoli, broken into flowerettes
1 cup seedless green grapes
1 cup seedless red grapes
1 cup sliced celery
1 bunch green onions, chopped

1/2 pound bacon, fried and crumbled
1 cup slivered almonds
1 cup mayonaise or Miracle Whip
1/4 cup sugar
2 Tbsp. vinegar

Mix together vegetables, fruit, bacon, and almonds. Blend together salad dressing, sugar and vinegar; mix with salad one hour before serving.

Marinated Carrot Salad

2 lb. carrots, cut in about 1 1/2-inch
    lengths or use baby carrots
1 green pepper, chopped
1 onion, chopped
1 can tomato soup
1 tsp. prepared mustard

1/2 cup oil
3/4 cup vinegar
1 tsp. Worcestershire sauce
1 cup sugar
1 tsp. salt

Cook carrots and cool. Add chopped green pepper and onion. Mix tomato soup, prepared mustard, oil, vinegar, Worcestershire suace, sugar and salt together and bring to a boil. Pour over vegetables. Marinate in the refrigerator for 24 hours. Drain off juice to serve. Save juice for storing leftovers. Keeps about three weeks in refrigerator.

My Mother-in-law's Vegetable Salad

1 head cauliflower, cut up
1 bunch broccoli, cut up
10 to 16 oz. frozen peas
1/2 cup chopped onion

1 pkg. Hidden Valley ranch dressing mix
1 cup sour cream
1 cup salad dressing

Combine ranch dressing mix with sour cream and salad dressing. Pour over chopped vegetables and chill overnight. This will keep for several days.

Crunchy Green Pea Salad

10 oz. frozen peas
1 cup sliced celery
1 cup cauliflower flowerettes
1/4 cup diced green onion
1/4 cup sliced pimento
1 cup roasted cashews

1/4 cup crisp-cooked, crumbled bacon
1/2 cup sour cream
1 cup Hidden Valley Ranch Dressing
1/2 tsp. Dijon style mustard
1 clove garlic, minced

Rinse frozen peas in hot water; drain. Combine peas with vegetables, cashews, bacon and sour cream. Mix together the dressing, mustard and garlic. Pour over salad. Toss gently.

Italian Dressing Broccoli Salad

1 bunch broccoli, cut up
1 head cauliflower, cut up (optional)
1 cup chopped onion
1 pint cherry tomatoes, sliced
4 to 6 ribs celery, sliced

1 or 2 cans water chestnuts, sliced
1 can pitted ripe olives, sliced
a few dashes oregano
1 bottle Italian dressing

Toss all ingredients together and refrigerate.

Cold Broccoli Salad

1 large fresh broccoli, cut in bite-sized
   pieces
3-4 green onions, sliced
1/2 lb. bacon, fried and crumbled

1 cup cheddar cheese, shredded
1/4 cup sugar
1/2 cup mayonnaise
1 Tbsp. vinegar

Blend sugar, mayonnaise and vinegar. Beat until creamy. Pour over other ingredients. Chill. Best if made several hours ahead.

Raw Cauliflower Salad

1 cup real mayonnaise
4 Tbsp. milk
1 small onion, grated
1 tsp. salt
1/4 tsp. lemon pepper

1 medium head cauliflower, broken into
   pieces
1 cup diced celery
1 pkg (10-16 oz.) frozen peas, uncooked
cheddar cheese, cubed or shredded

Mix mayonnaise, milk, onion, salt and lemon pepper. Add cauliflower, celery and frozen peas. Toss lightly. Top with cubed or shredded cheddar cheese. Chill.

Broccoli-Cauliflower Salad

1 head of cauliflower
1 bunch of broccoli
1 jar bacon bits
1/2 cup chopped onion

1/4 cup vinegar
1/3 cup sugar
1 cup salad dressing

Chop cauliflower and broccoli into small pieces. Mix together in large mixing bowl. Add bacon bits and onion. Set aside. In separate bowl, mix together vinegar, sugar and salad dressing until smooth. Pour dressing over broccoli and cauliflower mixture. Mix well. Refrigerate.

Another Broccoli-Cauliflower Salad

large head cauliflower, cut up (use stems)
large bunch broccoli, cut up (use stems and
    leaves)
2-3 green onions, sliced

10 oz. frozen peas
2 cups mayonnaise
1 cup sour cream
2 tsp. garlic powder

Blend mayonnaise, sour cream and garlic powder. Mix with all other ingredients. Salt and pepper to taste. Make ahead at least a few hours and chill. Keeps 2 to 3 days.

French Dressing

1 cup powdered sugar
1/2 cup ketchup
1/2 cup oil
1/4 cup vinegar

1 section garlic or garlic salt
1 tsp. grated onion or onion salt
1 tsp. worcestershire sauce
1/2 tsp. dry mustard

Mix together with an electric mixer for 10 minutes. (Can also be prepared in a food processor or blender.)

Lo-Cal French-Type Dressing

1/2 cup tomato juice
2 Tbsp. lemon juice
1/2 tsp. Worcestershire sauce
1/2 tsp. salt

1/2 tsp. dry mustard
1/4 tsp. garlic powder
1 tsp. sugar

Combine all ingredients well. Chill before serving. Makes about 3/4 cup dressing, 4 calories per tablespoon.

Bleu Cheese Dressing

1 quart real mayonnaise
1 tsp. garlic powder (not garlic salt)
3 oz. bleu cheese

1 cup buttermilk
1 tsp. parsley flakes

Mix together mayonnaise, buttermilk, garlic powder and parsley flakes. Crumble bleu cheese and fold in. Do not use electric mixer as the mayonnaise will separate. Refrigerate. Keeps for three weeks.

Roquefort Dressing

1 cup sour cream
1/4 cup mayonnaise
2 Tbsp. vinegar

1/2 cup salad oil
1/2 tsp. garlic salt
1 large wedge of Roquefort Bleu Cheese

Beat all ingredients in mixer, except cheese. When all is mixed well, add cheese (broken) and mix a few minutes longer. There will be cheese chunks left in mixture.

Pennsylvania Dutch Salad Dressing

1 egg
1/4 cup vinegar
1/3 cup water

2/3 cup sugar
1/2 Tbsp. corn starch
4 to 6 slices bacon, crisply fried

Whip egg in sauce pan. Add vinegar, water, sugar and cornstarch. Bring to rolling boil until it thickens. Fry bacon until crisp; drain on paper towel. Crumble bacon. Add warm salad dressing and crumbled bacon to lettuce, endive or other desired greens and toss. Serve immediately.

Pineapple Salad Dressing

1 cup pineapple juice
1/2 cup sugar
1 heaping Tbsp. flour

1 egg, beaten
pinch of salt

Bring juice to boil and add sugar, flour, and salt. Add some of the mixture to beaten egg. Pour mixture together, stir until thickened.

Thousand Island Dressing

1 cup mayonnaise
1/2 cup chili sauce
2 hard boiled eggs, chopped
2 Tbsp. green pepper, chopped
2 Tbsp. celery, chopped

1 1/2 Tbsp. finely chopped onion
1 tsp. paprika
1/2 tsp. salt
1/4 cup stuffed green olives, chopped

Combine all ingredients. Mix well. Makes 1 1/2 cups.

COLLEGE

Having grown up in a rural, small town area, going to college meant going to the big city of Minneapolis/St. Paul! Even though I'll always be a down-to-earth country girl, there's a part of me that thrills to see city lights and neon marquise signs, and to hear the music of an orchestra. I attended Bethel College in St. Paul and graduated in 1981 with a bachelor's degree in Speech Communications and minors in Business and Education. I almost became a teacher! Right before my senior year in college, I decided I'd rather be in television, so I never did my student teaching, although prior to that I had taught in five different schools while moving through the elementary education program.

I had two internships during my senior year. First, I interned as a communications assistant with Governor Al Quie, the republican governor of Minnesota. What a great experience! He was campaigning for a second term at the time, so I wrote a few of his speeches as well as traveled with the governor to campaign dinners. George Bush, then Vice President of the United States, came to the Twin Cities to help with the campaign, so I was able to meet him and take several photographs of the two men, since I was also a staff photographer. Unfortunately, he lost the election, so we all lost our jobs and I moved on.

My next internship was so important to my career. I interned as a reporter and assignment editor at the NBC affiliate, Channel 11, in Minneapolis. I worked hard for those six months to learn "news," and when I left, they helped me put together a resume tape. With that in hand, I had a "real" job within two weeks, being a news anchor/reporter at an ABC affiliate in Eau Claire, Wisconsin.

I made the most of those college years! I worked two part-time jobs through all four years. I was a secretary for the publicity department of the college and also waitressed at various restaurants. I also took a nine-month modeling course in the evening and had a few modeling jobs. I also took voice lessons from a professional opera singer for all four years of college.

Whew! It's amazing what you can do while young and full of energy! I also dated now and then. While most of my friends found their mates while in college, I graduated with no prospects. However, I knew the Lord had someone for me eventually, so decided to enjoy my independence in the meantime. Luckily, I didn't have to wait too long!

With my parents at my college graduation.

Vegetables

Vegetable Casserole

1 large bag (16-20 oz.) frozen mixed
   vegetables, any variety or combination
1 can cream of mushroom soup

8 oz. Velveeta cheese, cubed
3 cups soft bread crumbs
1/2 cup butter or margarine, melted

Combine vegetables, soup and cheese and put in shallow casserole or cake pan. Sprinkle bread crumbs over the casserole and then sprinkle the melted butter or margarine over the top. Bake at 350 degrees for 45-60 minutes.

Swiss Vegetable Medley

16 oz. bag frozen vegetables, such as
   broccoli, carrots, and cauliflower
1 can cream of mushroom soup
1 cup shredded Swiss cheese

1/3 cup sour cream
1/4 tsp. black pepper
4 oz. pimento, drained and chopped
1 can french fried onion rings

Combine vegetables, soup, 1/2 cup cheese, sour cream, pepper, pimento, and 1/2 can french fried onions. Pour into casserole. Bake covered at 350 degrees for 30 minutes. Top with remaining cheese and onion rings; bake uncovered 5 minutes longer.

Sauteed Vegetables

1/4 cup olive oil
6 cups vegetables (sliced yellow squash,
   zucchini, red pepper strips)

1 pkg. Italian salad dressing mix
1/4 cup red wine vinegar

Heat oil in large skillet on medium heat. Add vegetables; cook and stir until tender. Add salad dressing mix, toss to coat well. Stir in vinegar until well mixed. Serve warm. Makes 4-6 servings.

Microwaved Carrots

1 pound carrots
1/4 cup water
1 Tbsp. butter

1 Tbsp. brown sugar
1/2 to 1 tsp. dill

Peel carrots. Slice 1/4 " thick. Put in 1 quart casserole with water. Cover and cook on high in microwave for 7 minutes. Let stand 3 minutes; drain. Stir in butter, brown sugar and dill.

Company Carrots

2 cups cooked carrots, sliced
6 oz. cream cheese
1/2 can celery soup

1 cup bread crumbs
cheddar cheese

Mix together carrots, cream cheese and soup. Put into buttered dish. Top with bread crumbs and grated cheese. Heat through and serve.

Dress-Em-Up Carrots

1 cup cooked carrots
1 can pearl onions (or 1 cup fresh
   onions, cooked)
4 Tbsp. butter, melted

1/2 cup water
1 cup grated cheddar cheese
1 can cream of chicken soup
cracker crumbs

Place carrots, onions and soup in casserole and pour 1/2 cup water over. Top with cheese, butter and crumbs. Bake at 350 degrees for 30 minutes. Serves 8

Marinated Carrots

3 lbs. carrots, sliced, cooked and drained
1 large onion, sliced
1 large green pepper, sliced
1 can tomato soup
1 cup sugar

1/2 cup salad oil
3/4 cup vinegar
1/4 tsp. dillweed
1/2 tsp. pepper
1 tsp. salt

Combine all ingredients, except carrots, in saucepan; bring to boil. Boil 1 minute. Pour over carrots. Refrigerate and serve cold.

Freezer Corn

1 lb. butter
22 cups corn (Approx. 40 ears)

1 pint half & half
1 tsp. salt

Cut corn off ears. Mix all ingredients and bake in oven at 300 degrees for 1 hour. Stir every 15 minutes. Cool, package and freeze.

Scalloped Corn

2 cans cream-style corn
4 large or 5 small eggs
20 saltine crackers
1 corn can of milk

1/2 tsp. salt
1/4 tsp. pepper
dash MSG (optional)
seasoned salt to taste

Beat the eggs in casserole dish with fork. Add the 2 cans of cream style corn. Crush the saltine crackers and add to corn, along with seasonings. Fill one empty corn can with milk and mix into corn. Add several dabs of butter on the top and bake at 350 degrees for 90 minutes or until firm.

Green Bean and Bacon Casserole

2 (16 oz.) cans green beans, drained
1 can condensed cream of mushroom soup
3/4 cup milk
1 (2.8 oz.) can french fried onion rings

1 cup shredded cheddar cheese (optional)
2 oz. jar bacon bits (or bacon, fried and
    crumbled)
1/8 tsp. pepper

Combine all ingredients (using only half of the onion rings and bacon bits) and mix; pour into casserole. Bake 30 minutes at 350 degrees. Top with remaining onion rings and bacon bits. Bake 5 minutes longer.

Green Bean Casserole

1 can cream of mushroom soup
1/4 cup milk
1 tsp. soy sauce

1 can French fried onions
3 cups French style green beans, drained
dash of pepper

In a 1-quart casserole, stir soup, milk and soy sauce until smooth; mix in half of the onions, all the beans and the pepper. Bake in a 350 degree oven for 20 minutes or until bubbling. Top with remaining onions and bake 5 more minutes.

Asparagus Casserole

1 large can asparagus tips
1 can cream of mushroom soup
2 hard cooked eggs, sliced
2 cups cracker crumbs

1/2 lb. grated sharp cheddar cheese
1/2 cup margarine, melted
1/2 cup sliced almonds

Mix cheese and crumbs. Add asparagus liquid to soup. Butter bottom and sides of casserole dish. Put into dish in this order: 1/3 of crumb and cheese mixture, 1/2 of asparagus, 1/2 of soup mixture, 1/2 of melted margarine and 1 egg, sliced. Make a second layer exactly the same as the first. Finish with remaining 1/3 of crumb and cheese mixture; then sliced almonds. Bake 30 minutes at 350 degrees.

Baked Asparagus

1 lb. fresh asparagus
2 Tbsp. minced parsley

2 Tbsp. margarine, melted
2 Tbsp. olive oil

Layer asparagus in a 9x13-inch pan. Pour margarine and oil over asparagus. Sprinkle with parsley. Cover with foil. Bake at 375 degrees for 15 minutes.

Broccoli-Cauliflower Casserole

20 oz. pkg. frozen cauliflower
10 oz. pkg. frozen broccoli
1 can cream of celery soup

1 can cream of mushroom soup
8 oz. jar Cheese Whiz
french fried onion rings

Cook the cauliflower and broccoli until tender, but not mushy. Drain well. Mix cheese whiz and soups. Add vegetables. Bake uncovered at 350 degrees for 25 minutes. Put 1 can french fried onion rings on top and bake for 5 minutes more.

Carmelized Onions in Squash

2 small acorn squash
1/3 cup sugar
2 large onions, sliced

2 Tbsp. butter or margarine
1/2 tsp. finely shredded orange peel

Cut squash in half lengthwise. Remove seeds and strings. Place cut side down in a shallow pan. Bake 30 minutes at 350 degrees. Turn squash cut side up; bake 15 to 20 minutes more or until fork tender. Meanwhile, in a heavy skillet, heat sugar over medium heat until carmelized. Add onions, butter and shredded orange peel. Cook and stir 7-8 minutes until onions are tender and glazed. Spoon onions into squash halves and serve.

Celery Casserole

1/2 cup butter or margarine
1 small onion, chopped
2 cups chopped celery
1 can water chestnuts, sliced

1 can cream of mushroom or
   cream of chicken soup
1 cup bread crumbs
1 cup shredded cheddar cheese

Save 2 Tbsp. butter; saute onions and celery in the remaining butter. In baking dish, put sliced chestnuts, then celery and onion mixture. Pour soup over all. Sprinkle bread crumbs on top; dot with remaining 2 Tbsp. butter. Top with cheese. Bake at 350 degrees for 30 minutes. Cover with foil for the first 10-15 minutes, so the cheese doesn't melt too quickly. Serves 4-6.

Baked Frozen Peas

20 oz. frozen peas
1 can cream of celery soup

1/2 cup bread crumbs
4 Tbsp. melted butter

Butter a quart casserole, break up frozen peas and mix in soup. Top with buttered crumbs and bake uncovered for 45 minutes at 400 degrees.

Lemon Mint Peas

1 lb. frozen peas
1/2 lb. pearl onions
1 jar diced pimento, drained
1 1/2 Tbsp. butter

1 1/2 tsp. lemon juice
1 1/2 tsp. mint flakes
grated lemon rind

Cook the peas and the onions. Add the remaining ingredients and cook until butter melts.

Company Beets

2 Tbsp. brown sugar
1 Tbsp. cornstarch
1/4 tsp. salt
1 cup pineapple tidbits

1 Tbsp. butter
1 Tbsp. lemon juice
2 cups sliced cooked beets

Cook brown sugar, cornstarch and salt with pineapple (and juice) until thick, stirring constantly. Add butter, lemon juice and beets. Heat through.

Zucchini Casserole

6 cups thinly sliced zucchini
3 strips bacon, cut in small pieces
1 tsp. salt
1/8 tsp. pepper

1 cup sliced fresh or canned tomatoes
1 cup shredded cheddar cheese
1 Tbsp. flour

Fry bacon, add zucchini; cover and simmer 5 minutes. Add remaining ingredients and pour into a 1 1/2 quart casserole. Bake 30 to 35 minutes at 375 degrees.

Creamy Potatoes

2 lbs. frozen, diced hash browns
1 can cream of potato soup
1 can cream of celery soup
1/2 to 1 cup chopped onion
1/2 cup chopped green pepper

salt and pepper to taste
8 oz. sour cream
parsley flakes
paprika

Mix all ingredients except parsley and paprika and put into greased 9x13 pan. Sprinkle parsley flakes and paprika on top. Bake 1 1/2 to 2 hours at 300 degrees. Serves 12.

Butter Baked Taters

1/4 cup butter
3 Tbsp. minced green onion
3 large baking potatoes, peeled

salt and pepper to taste
2 Tbsp. grated parmesan cheese

Preheat oven to 500 degrees. Melt butter in small suacepan. Saute onion until tender, about 3 minutes. Halve potatoes lengthwise, then slice crosswise into 1/8- inch thick slices. Immediately line up in buttered 13x9" baking pan with slices overlapping. Pour butter mixture over potatoes. Season with salt and pepper. Bake 20 minutes. Remove from oven; sprinkle with parmesan cheese. Bake an additional 5 to 7 minutes or until cheese is melted and slightly browned.

Refrigerated Mashed Potatoes

5 lbs. potatoes, peeled, quartered,
*   cooked in salted water, drained*
*   and mashed*
6 oz. cream cheese
1 cup sour cream

2 tsp. onion salt
1 tsp. salt
1/4 tsp. pepper
2 Tbsp. margarine

Add all ingredients to mashed potatoes until fluffy. Bake at 350 degrees for 30 minutes in a greased 2-quart casserole, uncovered. After it is baked, you can place in refrigerator for as long as 2 weeks and use what you need. Need to bake for 45 minutes then or microwave until heated through.

Hash Brown Potato Casserole

2 lbs. frozen hash browns, thawed
1/4 cup melted butter
1 tsp. salt
1/2 tsp. pepper
1/4 cup chopped onion

2 cans cream of chicken soup
1 pint sour cream
2 cups shredded cheddar cheese
2 cups crushed corn flakes

Mix all ingredients and put in greased 9x13-inch pan. Sprinkle more cornflakes on top. Pour an additional 1/4 cup butter over top. Bake at 350 degrees for 45-55 minutes.

Roadhouse Potatoes

3 cups half and half cream
1/2 cup butter
1 tsp. salt

2 lb. frozen hash browns, thawed
1/2 cup grated parmesan cheese

Heat cream and butter. Add salt. Place potatoes in flat, greased glass 9x12-inch dish. Pour cream mixture over potatoes. Sprinkle cheese on top. Bake at 325 degrees for 1 hour.

Cheesy Scalloped Potatoes

6-7 potatoes, peeled & sliced
1 can cream of mushroom soup
1 can cream of chicken soup
1 soup can of milk (or water)
1 cup grated cheddar cheese

2 Tbsp. margarine
1 tsp. salt
1/4 tsp. pepper
1/4 tsp. seasoned salt
1/2 tsp. garlic powder

Place peeled and sliced potatoes in the bottom of a greased casserole. Dot with margarine. Combine all other ingredients and pour over potatoes. Bake at 375 degrees for 2 hours, stirring after 1 1/2 hours.

STARTING MY TV CAREER

5 - 4 - 3 - 2 - 1 - "ON AIR" - "LIVE!" When the red light appears on the camera, my adrenalin starts pumping! I grew up always wanting to be an actress on TV, but I knew in my heart I was a girl from a town of 2000 people in central Minnesota, so I would never have a chance at it. I learned to never say never!

When I got an internship at the Minneapolis NBC affiliate news department during my senior year in college, I was finally on my way to a career in television. That internship enabled me to get a job in TV news just two weeks after graduation. I was to be the first female news anchor at 6 and 10 PM, Monday through Friday, at WQOW-TV, the ABC affiliate in Eau Claire, Wisconsin. It was a smaller station, so I also was able to do reporting, editing, producing and some camera work. It was a great experience, but I wasn't sure I wanted to spend my life covering fires, murders, court cases, school board meetings, political conventions, union talks, etc.

After a few years in news, Mark and I were married, and we moved to Toronto, Canada, where I took acting classes and tried my hand at being an actress. I wasn't very good. The truth is that I'm much better at just being myself than pretending to be someone else. I was in the CBS mini-series, "Kane and Abel," and made about 30 television commercials, but that was it.

When we moved back to the States, none of the news stations were hiring, so I auditioned for CVN, the Cable Value Network. I was hired right away at the four-month-old cable shopping channel and started on the 3 AM to 6 AM shift. I literally learned how to make sales presentations "on the job." The most important lessons I learned were to have credibility and know exactly what I was talking about on each product and to be honest and genuine. These things are still most important to me in my job today.

I made a lot of friends at CVN which have continued to this day. It was a happy time and a perfect stepping stone to my terrific job at QVC.

On the job . . . at WQOW-TV, Channel 18, in Eau Claire, Wisc. (above) and at CVN in Minnesota (left and below).

Meats &
Main Dishes

15 Minute Beef Stroganoff

2 lb. ground beef
2/3 cup water
1 can cream of chicken soup
1 envelope onion soup mix

1 cup sour cream
2 Tbsp. flour
noodles or rice

Brown the meat. Add water and soups. Heat to boiling. Reduce heat. Blend sour cream and flour and add to the meat. Cook and stir until thick. Heat through but do not boil. Serve over rice or noodles.

Super Stew

Pot Roast Leftovers (beef, potatoes,
    carrots, onions)
2 cups water
2 beef bouillon cubes
1 1/2 tsp. Worcestershire Sauce

1/2 cup ketchup
10 oz. frozen mixed vegetables, if needed
2 cups Bisquick
2/3 cup milk

Mix all ingredients except Bisquick and milk. To make dumplings, mix Bisquick and milk and drop by spoonfuls onto stew. Cook, uncovered, over low heat, 10 minutes. Cover and cook 10 more minutes.

Beef Stew

Put in Nesco Roaster (4 or 6 qt.):
1 lb. beef stew meat, cut up
1 pkg. dried onion soup mix
1 can beef broth
1 can cream of mushroom soup
1 soup can of water

Add in desired amounts of:
carrots, peeled and chopped
potatoes, peeled and cut into chunks
onions, peeled and cut into chunks

Cook 3 hours at 300 degrees. Easy and good!

Minnesota Minnestroni

2 lbs. hamburger
1 cup chopped onion
1 clove garlic, minced
28 oz. can tomatoes
15 oz. can kidney beans
12 oz. can whole kernel corn
1 cup sliced celery
2 cups sliced zuchinni

1 cup uncooked macaroni
2 cups water
1 1/2 tsp. salt
1 1/2 tsp. Italian seasoning
2 tsp. instant beef bouillon
parmesan cheese
2 cups shredded cabbage

Cook and stir meat, onion and garlic until brown. Drain fat. Stir in tomatoes (with liquid), beans (with liquid), corn (with liquid), and remaining ingredients except cheese. Heat to boiling. Reduce heat, cover and stir occasionally until macaroni and vegetables are tender, about 30 minutes. Serve with cheese.

Hungarian Goulash

1 cup chopped onion
1 clove garlic, minced
2 lbs. round steak, cut in 1/2" cubes
2 Tbsp. flour
3/4 tsp. salt

1/4 tsp. pepper
1 tsp. paprika
1/8 tsp. dried thyme, crushed
1 bay leaf
14 1/2 oz. canned tomatoes

Put round steak, onion, and garlic in crock pot or Nesco roaster. Stir in flour and mix well to coat cubes. Add remaining ingredients. Cover and cook on low for 7-10 hours. Thirty minutes before serving, add 1 cup sour cream. Serve over noodles.

Monterrey Casserole

1 lb. ground beef, lightly browned
2 Tbsp. minced onion
3/4 tsp. seasoned salt

2-8 oz. can tomato sauce
4 cups taco flavored tortilla chips
2 cups shredded cheddar cheese

Mix together the ground beef, onion, seasoned salt and tomato sauce and simmer for 5 minutes. Put 3 cups tortilla chips in a 2-quart casserole. Sprinkle with 1 cup shredded cheddar cheese. Pour the meat sauce over the cheese. Top with remaining cheese. Sprinkle remaining tortilla chips over the top. Bake 15 minutes at 350 degrees. Garnish with ripe olives, if desired.

Hearty Beef 'N Potato Casserole

2 cups frozen tater tots
1 lb. ground beef, browned
10 oz. frozen chopped broccoli
1 can french fried onions
1 small tomato, chopped

1 can cream of celery coup
1/3 cup milk
1 cup shredded cheddar cheese
1/4 tsp. garlic powder
1/8 tsp. pepper

Place tater tots in casserole. Bake, uncovered, at 400 degrees for 10 minutes. Place browned ground beef on top of potatoes. Add broccoli, 1/2 can french fried onions and chopped tomato. Combine soup, milk, 1/2 cup cheese, garlic powder and pepper. Pour over beef mixture. Bake, covered, 20 minutes at 400 degrees. Top with 1/2 cup shredded cheese and the remaining 1/2 can of french fried onions. Bake, uncovered, 2 to 3 minutes longer.

Rice Hot Dish

1 lb. hamburger
1/2 cup diced onion
1 cup diced celery
1/2 cup uncooked rice

1 can cream of chicken soup
1 can cream of mushroom soup
1 can water
potato chips, crushed

Brown hamburger, onion and celery together. Combine with rice, soups and water and put in baking dish. Top with crushed potato chips, if desired. Bake about 90 minutes at 325 degrees. (Add water if it gets dry.)

Wild Rice Casserole

4 cups boiling water
1 1/3 cups wild rice
2 1/2 lbs. ground beef
1/2 cup chopped onions
2 cans cream of chicken soup
16 oz. canned mushrooms, plus liquid
1/2 cup hot water
1 tsp. salt

1/4 tsp. celery salt
1/4 tsp. onion powder
1/4 tsp. garlic powder
1/4 tsp. paprika
1/8 tsp. pepper
1 bay leaf, crushed
1/2 cup parmesan cheese

Mix boiling water with wild rice. Let stand 15-30 minutes; drain and set aside. Brown ground beef with onions and bay leaf; drain. Add all remaining ingredients, including rice, and pour into baking dish. Bake 1 hour, or a little more, at 350 degrees. Serves 12.

Hamburger-Noodle Bake for a Crowd

4 lbs. ground beef
1 or 2 lbs. link sausages, cut up
3 cups chopped onions
3 cups chopped celery
1 cup chopped green pepper
16 oz. medium noodles
3 cans (10 3/4 oz.) tomato soup
4 cups shredded American cheese

12 oz. bottle chili sauce
1/4 cup chopped pimento
2 tsp. salt
2 tsp. chili powder
1/2 tsp. pepper
2 cups water
4 1/2 cups soft bread crumbs
1/4 cup butter, melted

In a large skillet, cook beef, link sausage, onion, celery and green pepper, until ground beef is brown. Drain off fat. Cook noodles according to package directions; drain well. Return noodles to kettle. Stir in meat mixture, tomato soup, cheese, chili sauce, pimento, salt, chili powder, pepper and water. Mix well. Divide mixture between three 9x13" baking dishes. Toss bread crumbs with melted butter. Sprinkle atop casseroles. Bake, uncovered, at 350 degrees until heated through, about 45 minutes. Garnish with green pepper rings, if desired. Makes 3 casseroles, 12 servings each. May be frozen and baked at a later time, when that unexpected company arrives!

Tater Tot Hot Dish

2 lbs. hamburger, browned & seasoned
    to taste
1 pkg. dry onion soup mix

20 oz. frozen mixed vegetables
2 cans cream of mushroom soup
2 lb. bag frozen Tater Tots

In 9x13-inch pan, put browned hamburger on bottom; sprinkle dry onion soup mix over hamburger. Add vegetables and mushroom soup. Put Tater Tots on top and bake at 350 degrees for 1 1/2 to 2 hours.

Hamburger Cabbage Casserole

1 lb. lean ground beef
1 onion, chopped
1 cup tomato soup
3/4 tsp. salt

1/2 cup Minute Rice
1 small head cabbage, coarsely chopped
1/4 tsp. pepper

Cook rice; while it is standing, brown ground beef with salt, pepper and onions. Simmer until onions are tender. Add tomato soup and heat thoroughly. In a casserole, layer half of the cabbage, rice, and meat mixture, then repeat. Bake at 350 degrees for 1 hour.

Hamburger Chili Macaroni

1 lb. ground beef
6 oz. can tomato paste
3 cups hot water
1 cup chopped onion

1 tsp. chili powder
1 tsp. salt
1/4 tsp. garlic salt
2 cups elbow macaroni, uncooked

Brown beef and onions; pour off excess fat. Add tomato paste, water and seasonings. Bring to a boil. Add macaroni; cover and simmer 15 minutes. Serves 4 to 6.

Cheese-Topped Beef and Potato Bake

1 1/2 lbs. ground beef
1 medium onion, diced
1 medium stalk celery, diced
32 oz. tomato sauce
4 oz. mushrooms, sliced
1/2 cup water

3/4 tsp. salt
1/2 tsp. sugar
1/4 tsp. pepper
3 medium potatoes, thinly sliced
4 oz. shredded mozzarella cheese

Cook beef, onion, and celery until browned. Stir in tomato sauce, mushrooms, water, salt, sugar and pepper. Heat to boiling; reduce heat to low. Cover and simmer 5 minutes. Into a 9x13-inch baking dish, spoon 1/3 of beef mixture. Arrange 1/2 of potato slices on top. Repeat, ending with ground beef mixture. Cover dish with foil. Bake in 375 degree oven for 1 hour or until potatoes are tender. Remove from oven. Discard foil. Sprinkle with cheese. Return to oven just until cheese melts.

Hamburger Hotdish (Rice Chow Mein)

1 lb. hamburger
1 onion, chopped
1 can cream of chicken soup
1 can cream of mushroom soup
1/2 cup dry rice, not cooked
4 oz. can mushroom pieces, drained

1 cup diced celery
2 soup cans of water
2 Tbsp. worcestershire sauce
2 Tbsp. soy sauce
chow mein noodles

Brown hamburger and onion together. Mix in remaining ingredients except chow mein noodles and put in casserole. Bake in 350 degree oven for 1 hour. Put chow mein noodles over the top and bake 1/2 hour more at 300 degrees.

Stuffed Green Peppers

6 green peppers
1 1/2 lbs. ground beef
1/2 cup diced onion
1 can stewed tomatoes
1 Tbsp. worcestershire sauce
1 tsp. pepper

2 Tbsp. butter
1 tsp. salt
1 cup minute rice, cooked
3/4 cup buttered soft bread crumbs
8 oz. shredded cheddar cheese

Cut off tops of green peppers; clean out seeds. Boil peppers for 5 minutes in salt water; set aside. Brown onions and ground beef, then add rest of ingredients, except bread crumbs and cheese. Simmer for several minutes. Put mixture into peppers. Top with bread crumbs. Put in a covered baking dish. Bake 45 minutes at 375 degrees. Sprinkle cheese on top and bake for 10 more minutes, uncovered.

Sauerkraut Hamburger Casserole

2 cups macaroni noodles, uncooked
1 lb. hamburger
1/2 cup chopped onion
1/2 cup shredded cheddar cheese

1 can cream of mushroom soup
1 can cream of celery soup
11 oz. sauerkraut

Brown hamburger with onion; season to taste. Mix all ingredients together. Put into greased casserole dish. Bake at 350 degrees for 30 minutes. Note: Double this recipe fits perfectly in the 4-quart Nesco Roaster.

Souper Meat and Potato Pie

1 can cream of mushroom soup
1 pound ground beef
1/4 cup onion, finely chopped
1 egg, slightly beaten
1/4 cup fine dry bread crumbs

2 Tbsp. chopped parsley
1/4 tsp. salt
dash of pepper
2 cups mashed potatoes
1/4 cup shredded mild cheese

Preheat oven to 350 degrees. Mix thoroughly 1/2 cup soup, beef, onion, egg, bread crumbs, parsley, and seasonings. Press firmly into 9-inch pie plate. Bake at 350 degrees for 25 minutes; spoon off fat. Frost with potatoes; top with remaining soup and cheese. Bake 10 minutes more or until done. Garnish with cooked sliced bacon, if desired.

Company Casserole

1 lb. ground beef	8 oz. egg noodles
1/2 tsp. garlic powder	8 oz. sour cream
1/2 tsp. salt	8 oz. cottage cheese
dash pepper	8 oz. cream cheese, softened
15 oz. can tomato sauce	3 medium green onions, chopped

Brown ground beef; add salt, pepper and garlic powder. Simmer 30 minutes in tomato sauce. Mix sour cream, cream cheese and cottage cheese well with fork. Add finely chopped onion and mix. Cook noodles as directed on package; drain and add 2 Tbsp. butter. In a casserole, start with a bit of the meat sauce, then layer of noodles, layer of cheese mix. Repeat layers, ending with meat sauce. Bake uncovered at 350 degrees for about 45 minutes. Serve with tossed green salad and garlic bread.

Lasagna

16 oz. pkg. lasagna noodles	2 lb. grated mozzarella cheese
2 Tbsp. cooking oil	24 oz. cottage cheese
4 or 5 cloves garlic	1 lb. ground beef, browned
32 oz. jar spaghetti sauce	salt and pepper to taste

Boil noodles as directed on package. Add oil to boiling water to keep noodles from sticking. Let cool about 10 minutes until easy to handle. Thinly chop garlic and add to spaghetti sauce. Spray large roasting pan (or 4-quart Nesco roaster) with vegetable cooking oil. Lay out 1 layer of noodles on bottom of pan and sprinkle in cheese, bits of hamburger and spoonfuls of cottage cheese. Add enough spaghetti sauce to cover most parts lightly. Repeat layers until out of ingredients. Top layer should end with sauce, meat and cheese over noodles. Cover pan and bake at 350 degrees for 1 hour. Serves 8 very hungry people.

Mary Beth's Favorite Lasagne

1 lb. ground beef
32-40 oz. spaghetti sauce
12 lasagne noodles
4 cups ricotta cheese (or small
*   curd cottage cheese)*
4 cups shredded mozzarella cheese

1/4 cup grated parmesan cheese
4 eggs
1 Tbsp. chopped parsley
1 tsp. salt
1/4 tsp. pepper

Brown the ground beef and drain off fat. Add the spaghetti sauce, salt and pepper to the ground beef. Set aside. Cook lasagne noodles according to package directions and set aside. Mix together the remaining ingredients (except for 2 cups of the mozzarella cheese); then, in a long rectangular pan or cake pan, lightly greased, or 4-qt. Nesco roaster, place a layer of noodles (4) in the bottom of the pan, cover with 1/3 of the meat sauce, then 1/2 of the cheese mixture, then 4 more noodles, 1/3 of the meat sauce, 1/2 of the cheese mixture, then last 4 noodles and the remaining meat sauce. Top with 2 cups of shredded mozzarella cheese. Cook 45 minutes at 350 degrees. Let it set for a couple minutes before cutting to serve.

Carefree Lasagne

1 lb. lasagne noodles, uncooked
24 oz. cottage cheese
1/2 cup parmesan cheese
1 Tbsp. parsley flakes
3/4 lb. grated mozzarella cheese
4 cups tomatoes (or sauce plus tomatoes
*   to equal 4 cups)*
2 tsp. salt

1 1/2 Tbsp. onion flakes
1/2 tsp. garlic powder
2 lbs. hamburger, browned, drained
2 cups tomato paste
3 cups water
1 tsp. sugar
1 tsp. oregano

Mix browned hamburger with tomatoes, salt, onion flakes, garlic powder, tomato paste, water, sugar and oregano. In separate bowl mix cottage cheese, parmesan cheese, parsley flakes and mozzarella cheese. In two 9x13-inch pans, layer sauce alternately with uncooked lasagne noodles and cheese mixture. End with meat sauce on top. Cover with a layer of waxed paper and seal tightly with aluminum foil Bake at 350 degrees for 1 hour, 45 minutes. Let stand, covered, for 30 minutes before serving.

Porcupine Meatballs

1 1/2 lb. ground beef
1/2 cup raw rice
1 cup chopped onion
2/3 cup milk

1 tsp. salt
1/4 tsp. pepper
1 can (10 1/2 oz.) tomato soup
3/4 cup water

Mix well the ground beef, rice, onion, milk, salt and pepper. Drop by tablespoonfuls in 9x13" pan. Set aside. Combine soup and water. Pour sauce over meatballs. Cover pan tightly with aluminum foil. Bake at 350 degrees for one hour.

Swedish Meatballs

1 lb. hamburger
1 egg
1/2 cup dry bread crumbs
1 can cream of mushroom soup
1 can cream of chicken soup

1/2 cup chopped onion
1 cup sour cream
2 Tbsp. butter
1/2 cup chopped green pepper
salt and pepper

Mix hamburger, egg, bread crumbs, salt and pepper to taste; form into meatballs. Cook in skillet on low to medium heat until done. Drain any grease. Add butter, onion and green pepper and cook another 2-3 minutes. In separate bowl, combine the soups and sour cream together and mix. Turn heat down on low and add the soup mixture. Let simmer on low for 20 minutes. Serve with rice or potatoes.

Scandinavian Meatballs

2 lb. ground sirloin
1/4 cup chopped onions
4 eggs
1 1/4 cups bread crumbs
1 tsp. nutmeg
1/2 tsp. cinnamon
1/2 tsp. all spice

1 tsp. seasoned salt
1 tsp. salt
1 quart milk
3/4 cup flour
3/4 cup melted butter
1/2 tsp. cinnamon
1/2 tsp. nutmeg

Combine ground sirloin, onions, eggs, bread crumbs, 1 tsp. nutmeg, 1/2 tsp. cinnamon, all spice, seasoned salt, and salt. Roll into meat balls and bake in 375 degree oven until browned. Boil the milk. Combine flour with butter and add to milk. Add 1/2 tsp. cinnamon and 1/2 tsp. nutmeg. Cook until slightly thickened. Put browned meat balls in the sauce and let simmer for 15 minutes.

Sharon's Meat Loaf

1 1/2 lbs. hamburger
3/4 cup oatmeal
1 cup milk
1 egg
1 small onion, chopped

1 Tbsp. Worcestershire sauce
1 1/2 tsp. salt
1/2 tsp. dry mustard
1/4 tsp. pepper
1/4 tsp. sage

Mix ingredients together and spread in ungreased loaf pan.   Top with a mixture of 1/2 cup catsup, 2 Tbsp. mustard and 2 Tbsp. brown sugar. Bake at 350 degrees for 90 minutes.

Dad's Easy Meatloaf

3 lbs. hamburger
1 cup oatmeal
1 cup cracker crumbs
1 can vegetable soup
1 can tomato sauce or puree

2 Tbsp. dried onions
1 Tbsp. soy sauce
3 eggs, slightly beaten
1 tsp. salt
ketchup

Mix all ingredients, except ketchup; put in pan. Put ketchup on top. Bake 1 1/2 hours at 350 degrees.

Faith's Meatloaf

2 lbs. ground beef
2 eggs
1 1/2 cups bread crumbs (or 30 saltine
   cracker squares, crushed)

3/4 cup ketchup
1 tsp. Accent
1/2 cup warm water
1 pkg. dry onion soup mix

Beat all ingredients together except the ground beef. Add ground beef to mixture. Put into loaf pan. Bake 1 hour at 350 degrees.

Pizza Meatloaf

1 can tomato soup
1/4 cup water
1/2 tsp. ground oregano
1 garlic clove, minced
1 cup bread crumbs
1/4 cup chopped onions

2 Tbsp. chopped parsley
1 egg, beaten
1 tsp. salt
1/8 tsp. pepper
2 lbs. ground beef
2 slices processed cheese

Blend soup, water, oregano and garlic. In bowl, combine 1/4 cup soup mixture, bread, onion, parsley, egg, salt and pepper. Mix thoroughly with ground beef. Shape firmly into a loaf; place in shallow baking pan. Bake at 350 degrees for 1 hour and 15 minutes. Remove from oven; spoon off fat. Pour remaining soup mixture over loaf. Top with cheese; bake until cheese melts. Serves 4 to 6.

Easy Chili

1 lb. hamburger
1/4 cup chopped onion
1/3 cup catsup
1/4 cup water
1/8 cup chopped celery
1 Tbsp. lemon juice
1/2 Tbsp. brown sugar
3/4 tsp. Worcestershire sauce

3/4 tsp. salt
1/2 tsp. vinegar
1/4 tsp. MSG
1/8 tsp. dry mustard
1 can kidney beans, including liquid
8 oz. tomato sauce
2 tsp. chili powder

Brown hamburger with onion; drain off excess fat. Add remaining ingredients and heat.

Chili Con Carne

1 lb. lean ground beef
1 medium onion, chopped
1 small green pepper, diced
2 large garlic cloves, minced

1 can tomatoes (14.5 to 16 oz.)
2 Tbsp. chili powder (or more, if desired)
1/2 tsp. salt
1 can kidney beans (or pinto beans)

In a 3-quart T-FAL sauce pan, cook ground beef, onion, green pepper and garlic over medium heat until onion is tender, about 10 minutes. Add tomatoes and their liquid, chili powder and salt. Heat to a boil. Reduce heat to low, cover and simmer 1 hour, stirring constantly. Stir in beans and their liquid; heat thoroughly. Serve in soup bowls with a choice of accompaniments (minced onion, chopped coriander, fresh chilies, shredded Monterey Jack or cheddar cheese.)

Texas Style Chili (No Beans)

4-5 lbs. boneless beef chuck
1/4 cup salad oil
2 large chopped onions
4 green peppers, diced
5 garlic cloves, crushed
2 - 28 oz. cans tomatoes
1 - 12 oz. can tomato paste

1/2 cup chili powder
1/4 cup sugar
2 Tbsp. salt
1 Tbsp. oregano
1 tsp. crushed pepper
3 cups water
shredded Monterey Jack cheese for garnish

Cut beef into half-inch cubes. Then, in dutch oven or stock pot, heat salad oil and add beef, in batches if necessary, until browned on all sides. With a slotted spoon, remove meat and set aside. Cook onions, green pepper and garlic for 10 minutes over medium heat, stirring occasionally. Return meat to pan and add tomatoes and their liquid and remaining ingredients except cheese. Heat to boiling. Reduce heat to low; cover and simmer for 1 1/2 to 2 hours or until meat is fork tender, stirring occasionally. Spoon chili into soup bowls; sprinkle shredded cheese over top for garnish.

Diane's Chili

2 lb. ground beef
1 clove garlic or garlic powder
2 large onions, chopped
1 1/2 tsp. salt
2-3 Tbsp. chili powder
1/4 tsp. red pepper (cayenne)
dash of cloves

2 cans kidney beans, plus juice
1/4 tsp. black pepper
1 tsp. paprika
1 tsp. basil
4 cups tomato juice
1 can crushed tomatoes

Brown ground beef with garlic and onions. Add remaining ingredients; simmer, uncovered, for 30 minutes.

Faith's Chili

2 lbs. ground beef
2 tsp. salt
1 Tbsp. garlic powder
dash pepper

3 cans hot chili beans
15 oz. tomato sauce
1/2 of a packet of chili seasoning mix
1 cup shredded cheddar cheese
mushrooms

Brown ground beef with salt, pepper and garlic powder. Add remaining ingredients and simmer about 15 minutes. This is a thicker, less tomato-tasting chili. Add a little water if too thick.

Calico Beans

1/2 lb. bacon, diced
1 lb. hamburger
1 Tbsp. prepared mustard
1 tsp. salt
1/2 cup chopped onion
1/2 cup brown sugar

1/2 cup ketchup
2 Tbsp. vinegar
2 lb. lima beans
15 oz. kidney beans
32 oz. pork & beans in tomato sauce
15 oz. butter beans

Brown bacon; drain on paper towels. Brown hamburger and onion; drain fat. Mix bacon and remaining ingredients, except beans, with the hamburger. Drain lima beans, kidney beans and butter beans; rinse. Add all the beans, including the pork and beans (with juice) to the hamburger. Bake uncovered at 300 degrees for 90 minutes. Serves 15. This works great in the Nesco roaster.

Ranch Baked Bean Casserole

1 lb. ground beef
1 pkg. dry onion soup mix
1/2 cup water
1 cup ketchup

2 Tbsp. prepared mustard
2 tsp. vinegar
32 oz. pork and beans
16 oz. kidney beans, drained

Brown the ground beef in a large skillet. Stir in the remaining ingredients and pour into a 2-quart casserole. Bake at 400 degrees for 30 minutes. 10 to 12 servings.

Taco Casserole

1 lb. hamburger
1/2 bottle taco sauce
1 cup frozen corn
crushed Doritos

2 cups cooked shell macaroni (1 cup uncooked)
2 cups grated cheddar cheese

Brown hamburger. Drain off fat. Add taco sauce, corn and cooked macaroni; cook 5 to 10 minutes. Put in casserole. Cover with grated cheese and top with crushed Doritos. Bake 20-30 minutes at 350 degrees.

Taco Crepe Filling

1 lb. ground beef
2 Tbsp. chopped onions
1 tsp. garlic salt
1 tsp. cumin
2 tsp. chili powder

1/2 tsp. crushed red pepper (optional)
taco sauce
grated cheese
sliced ripe olives
shredded lettuce

Brown ground beef and onions in small frypan. Drain grease. Add seasonings and simmer. Spoon mixture onto crepe and fold. Top with taco sauce. Garnish with grated cheese, shredded lettuce, and sliced ripe olives. (Works well with Cornmeal Crepe.)

Crazy Crust Pizza

1 1/2 lb. ground beef
1 cup flour
1 tsp. salt
1 tsp. oregano
1/8 tsp. pepper
2 eggs

2/3 cup milk
1 cup mushrooms
1/4 cup onion, chopped
1 cup pizza sauce
1 cup shredded mozzarella cheese

Brown ground beef; drain. Grease 12" pizza pan. Combine flour, salt, oregano, pepper, eggs, and milk. Mix until smooth. Pour batter into pan to cover bottom. Arrange topping of meat, mushrooms and onions. Drizzle on pizza sauce (or 1 can tomato sauce plus 2 tsp. oregano and 1/4 tsp. pepper.) Sprinkle with cheese. Bake 25-30 minutes at 425 degrees until crust is brown.

Upside Down Pizza

1 pound sausage
32 oz. jar spaghetti sauce
1 lb. mozzarella cheese
2/3 cup flour

1/2 tsp. salt
1/2 cup milk
2 eggs

Brown sausage; add spaghetti sauce. Pour the sausage and sauce into a 9x13 greased pan. Top with 1/2 pound mozzarella cheese. Mix together the flour, salt, milk and eggs; beat well. Top cheese with flour mixture. Add on top of flour mixture another 1/2 pound of cheese. Bake at 350 degrees for 25 minutes.

Easy Pizza

1 or 2 pkg. Pillsbury biscuits
1 cup sour cream
1 lb. hamburger
1/2 cup chopped onions

Italian seasoning to taste
salt and pepper to taste
15 oz. tomato sauce
1 cup mozzarella cheese

Spread biscuits on bottom of 9x13-inch pan. Spread sour cream over biscuits. Brown hamburger with onions, Italian seasoning, salt and pepper. Drain and pour over sour cream. Add tomato sauce and top with mozzarella cheese. Bake at 350 degrees for 30 minutes.

Pizza Casserole

1 1/2 lbs. hamburger
1 onion, chopped
1 green pepper, chopped
1/4 tsp. pepper
32 oz. jar spaghetti sauce
dash garlic powder

3/4 tsp. salt
1 tsp. oregano
1 Tbsp. parsley flakes
8 oz. spaghetti noodles, broken and cooked
3 cups shredded mozzarella cheese

Brown hamburger with onion and green pepper; drain. Add remaining ingredients, except noodles and cheese, and simmer 10 minutes. Add spaghetti noodles. Pour 1/2 of the mixture into baking dish. Top with 1 1/2 cups cheese. Pour remaining mixture over cheese and top with remaining 1 1/2 cups cheese. Bake at 375 degrees for 30 minutes.

Palermo Spaghetti Sauce

3 lb. ground beef
1 tsp. salt
1 tsp. pepper
2 Tbsp. oregano
1 Tbsp. parsley leaves
2 Tbsp. basil
1 cup chopped onion

1 tsp. garlic salt
4 cups tomato puree
1 cup tomato paste
3 cups water
1 Tbsp. sugar
2 Tbsp. parmesan cheese

Brown ground beef in hot oil for about 10 minutes. Add salt, pepper, oregano, basil, parsley flakes, onion and garlic salt. Saute for 10 minutes, stirring occasionally. Place in a pot with tomato puree, paste and water, sugar and cheese. Simmer for 2 to 3 hours, stirring occasionally, uncovered. Serves 10 to 12, depending on appetites. May be frozen when complete.

Italian Spaghetti Sauce

3 lb. ground beef
1 onion, chopped
1 tsp. salt
46 oz. can tomato juice
pinch garlic salt
1 Tbsp. sugar
1 green pepper, chopped

1 can condensed tomato soup
8 oz. can tomato sauce
6 oz. can tomato paste
1 cup chopped celery
dash chili powder
pinch of cloves
pinch of allspice

Brown ground beef and onion and salt. Drain off fat. Add the remaining ingredients and simmer for 2 hours. Add mushrooms, if desired. Serve over spaghetti noodles.

Soup-Burgers

1 lb. ground beef
1 egg, slightly beaten
1/3 cup dry bread crumbs

1 can condensed beefy-mushroom soup
French fried onions

Combine ground beef, egg and bread crumbs. Shape into 4 patties, brown on both sides. Pour condensed soup over burgers; cover and simmer 20 minutes. Top with canned French fried onions.

Beef with Sour Cream

1 lb. lean round steak
1/4 cup flour
1/4 tsp. salt
dash pepper
dash garlic powder
2 Tbsp. vegetable oil

3/4 cup chopped onions
1 cup beef broth
1/2 tsp. thyme
4 oz. can mushrooms, plus liquid
10 oz. frozen peas
1/2 cup sour cream

Remove bone and fat from round steak. Cut into thin, narrow strips. Combine flour, salt, pepper and garlic powder; dredge meat in flour mixture. Using a large skillet, quickly brown meat on all sides in vegetable oil. Add onions, beef broth, thyme and liquid from canned mushrooms. Cover and simmer about 45 minutes or until meat is tender. Add mushrooms and peas. Cover and cook 5-7 minutes. Stir in sour cream. Heat but do not boil. Serve on hot rice.

Beef Broccoli Stir Fry

1 lb. steak
2 Tbsp. soy sauce
1 tsp. salt
2 Tbsp. vegetable oil
1/2 tsp. baking soda
3 slices fresh ginger root
1/2 bunch green onions, chopped

1/2 cup chopped sweet onion
1 bunch fresh broccoli, cut up
3 Tbsp. oil
1 Tbsp. oyster sauce
2 Tbsp. soy sauce
1 tsp. corn starch
3 Tbsp. water

Cut steak into thin slices (easily done if cut when partially frozen.) Marinate in a mixture of 2 Tbsp. soy sauce, salt, 2 Tbsp. vegetable oil and baking soda. Blanch broccoli for one minute. Heat 3 Tbsp. oil in wok. Put in ginger root and green onions; cook 2 minutes. Add beef; cook until meat is not red. Take beef mixture out of wok; set aside. Cook chopped sweet onion in wok; add broccoli and continue to cook until onions are transparent. Add meat mixture; cook 2 minutes. Combine oyster sauce, 2 Tbsp. soy sauce, corn starch and water; add to wok and cook 2 more minutes. Serve with rice.

Stir Fried Beef and Vegetables

2 beef bouillon cubes
1/3 cup water
1/4 cup soy sauce
2 Tbsp. cider vinegar
2 1/2 tsp. cornstarch
1 tsp. sugar
vegetable oil

2 cloves garlic, halved
1 lb. flank steak, cut into 1/8" diagonal
    slices
1 large onion, sliced 1/4" thick
2 cups mushrooms, sliced 1/4" thick
2 medium green peppers, chopped
8 oz. can water chestnuts, sliced

In small saucepan, over low heat, dissolve bouillon cubes and water. Combine soy sauce, vinegar, cornstarch and sugar and stir into bouillon mixture. Set aside. In large skillet or wok, heat 2 Tbsp. oil over high heat. Add garlic cloves and cook a few seconds. Add steak and stir fry 2 minutes. Remove meat and juices; discard garlic. Wipe pan. Heat 1 Tbsp. oil and add onion, mushrooms, green peppers and water chestnuts. Stir fry 2 minutes over high heat. Add meat and juices, then bouillon mixture. Stir. Cover and cook 2 minutes. Stir and serve. Works great in T-Fal wok.

Bette Ball's Veal Veronique

1 1/2 lb. veal scaloppine (or chicken)
3 tsp. butter
1 tsp. onion, finely chopped
1/4 tsp. garlic powder
3/4 cup white wine

1 tsp. flour
1/2 lb. seedless grapes
1 cup heavy cream, whipped
salt and cayenne to taste
white rice

Tenderize veal with mallot or fork. Cut across grain into 1/2" strips. Saute onion in butter; add garlic powder. Add veal and saute 5 minutes. Remove veal and onion. Add wine to pan and boil 3 minutes. Sprinkle veal lightly with flour. Return veal to pan with grapes and simmer until juice is slightly thickened. Add cream and warm through. Season with salt and cayenne. Serve over white rice. A perfect candlelight dinner for four.

Corned Beef Dinner

6 oz. shell macaroni, cooked
12 oz. corned beef, chopped in cubes
4 oz. cheddar cheese, grated or cubed
1 can cream of chicken soup

1 cup milk
1/4 cup chopped onion
3/4 cup crushed potato chips
1/4 cup butter or margarine, melted

Cook macaroni as directed on package; drain. Combine macaroni, corned beef, cheese, soup, milk and onion in baking dish. Top with potato chips and sprinkle melted butter over the top. Bake 1 hour at 375 degrees.

Reuben Casserole

1 lb. can sauerkraut, drained
2 medium tomatoes, sliced
2 Tbsp. thousand island dressing
2 Tbsp. butter
corned beef

Swiss cheese
1 can refrigerator biscuits
2 rye crackers, crushed
1/4 tsp. caraway seed

Grease a 12x8-inch pan. Spread sauerkraut in bottom of dish. Top with tomato slices. Dot with dressing and butter. Cover with corned beef. Cut up cheese and put on top. Bake at 425 degrees for 15 minutes. Remove from oven; separate biscuits and place on top of casserole. Sprinkle with crackers and caraway seed. Bake at 425 degrees for 15 to 20 minutes or until biscuits are baked.

Breast of Chicken Magnifique

4 whole chicken breasts, about 3 lbs, split
1/4 cup butter or margarine
2 cups sliced mushrooms
2 cans cream of chicken soup

1 large clove garlic, minced
generous dash crushed thyme
1/8 tsp. rosemary, crushed
2/3 cup light cream

In a large skillet, brown the chicken in butter; remove. Brown mushrooms. Stir in soup, garlic, and seasonings; add chicken. Cover and cook over low heat 45 minutes. Stir now and then. Blend in cream; heat slowly. Serve with wild rice mix. Garnish with toasted, slivered almonds. 8 servings

Tex-Mex Chicken

4-6 boneless chicken breasts
1/2 cup Miracle Whip

1/4 cup salsa
1 tsp. chili powder

Mix Miracle Whip, salsa and chili powder. Stir in chicken breasts to coat. Broil 5 minutes on first side, 4-5 minutes on second side.

Chicken Piccata

1 lb. boneless chicken breasts
3/4 cup flour
1/2 tsp. oregano
vegetable oil
1/4 cup chicken broth
1 lemon sliced, or 1 Tbsp. lemon juice

1/4 tsp. salt
1/4 tsp. black pepper
2 cloves garlic, minced
1/4 cup white wine or apple juice
1/4 cup water

Mix flour, oregano, salt and pepper. Coat chicken breasts with flour mixture. Saute garlic in a little vegetable oil. Add chicken and brown on both sides. Add wine or apple juice, chicken broth, and water. Cook on medium heat for 10 minutes. Add lemon and cook 5 minutes more.

Oven Fried Chicken Parmesan

1 cup flour	2 eggs
1/4 tsp. pepper	3 Tbsp. milk
2 tsp. salt	1/3 cup fine dry bread crumbs
2 tsp. paprika	2/3 cup parmesan cheese

Preheat oven to 400 degrees. In first bowl, combine flour, pepper, salt, and paprika. In second bowl, beat eggs with milk. In third bowl, mix bread crumbs and parmesan cheese. Cut up chicken and coat pieces with contents of 3 bowls in order. Let stand 10 minutes. Put skin side down in large baking pan. Bake 30 minutes; turn chicken pieces over. Bake 30 minutes more on second side.

Lemon-Baked Chicken

2 Tbsp. oil or melted margarine	1/2 tsp. salt
3 Tbsp. fresh lemon juice	dash pepper
1 clove garlic, crushed	3 lbs. chicken, cut into serving pieces

Preheat oven to 350 degrees. Combine ingredients, except chicken. Arrange chicken in shallow casserole or baking pan. Pour lemon mixture over chicken. Cover and bake until tender, about 40 minutes, basting occasionally. Uncover and bake 10 minutes longer. To serve, sprinkle with chopped parsley.

Chicken Baked in Honey

1/8 cup honey	1/2 Tbsp. lemon juice
1/8 cup prepared mustard	6 pieces of frying chicken

Preheat oven to 350 degrees. Combine honey, mustard and lemon juice. Butter bottom of 9x9" square pan. Add chicken. Season with salt and pepper. Top with honey mixture. Bake for 30 minutes. Turn and bake 30 minutes more.

Chicken With Dill & Vegetables

1 medium green pepper, chopped
1 medium red pepper, chopped
1 medium zucchini, sliced
1 large onion, quartered

1 Tbsp. oil
2 chicken breasts, split
1 Tbsp. chopped fresh dill
salt and pepper to taste

Heat the oil in a large skillet. Quickly saute chicken in hot oil for several minutes until golden on both sides. Add the dill, salt and pepper and vegetables. Turn the heat to low and cover. Simmer 45 minutes or until tender. Works great in T-Fal Chicken Fryer!

Gingered Chicken

1/4 cup flour
1/2 tsp. ginger
1/4 tsp. salt
boneless chicken pieces
2 Tbsp. butter or margarine

1/2 cup onion, chopped
1 cup chicken broth
3/8 cup milk
1 Tbsp. chopped crystallized ginger

Mix flour, ginger and salt. Dredge chicken pieces in flour mixture and reserve remaining mixture. Melt butter and brown chicken pieces 3 minutes on each side. Remove to platter. Brown onion for 3 minutes. Stir in reserved flour. Gradually add chicken broth; bring to boil and cook 5 minutes. Add milk and crystallized ginger. Add chicken to sauce and cook until fork tender. Serve with sauce.

Honey Mustard Chicken a la Zip

Mix: 1/4 cup Miracle Whip
1 Tbsp. Dijon mustard

1 Tbsp. honey

Spread mixture on boneless, split chicken breasts. Broil 5 minutes on each side.

Easy Skillet-Roasted Chicken

2 Tbsp. flour
1/4 tsp. ground sage
1/4 tsp. dried thyme
4-6 pieces chicken

2 Tbsp. margarine or butter
1 can cream of chicken soup
1/2 cup water
hot cooked rice

In a bowl or on waxed paper, combine flour, sage and thyme. Coat chicken pieces lightly with flour mixture. In a skillet, over medium heat, melt margarine/butter and cook chicken 10 minutes or until browned on both sides. Remove chicken to platter. Add soup and water to skillet, stirring to loosen browned bits. Reduce heat to low. Add chicken, cover, and simmer 5 minutes or until chicken is tender. Serve over rice. Garnish with fresh thyme if desired.

Crispy Garlic Chicken

3 lb. broiler-frying chicken
garlic powder
paprika

salt and pepper
1 large onion

Preheat oven to 350 degrees. Wash chicken and cut into serving pieces. Pat dry with paper towels; put on waxed paper. Sprinkle generously with salt and pepper, garlic powder and paprika. With fingers, rub the seasonings into the chicken. Peel and slice onion. Arrange slices on bottom of ungreased casserole. Arrange chicken pieces over onion slices. Bake one hour. Good with rice or broccoli.

Hunter Style Chicken

4 slices bacon
1 medium onion, sliced
1 lb. can tomatoes, cut up
1 Tbsp. sugar

2-3 lbs. chicken pieces
salt and pepper
1/2 cup Heinz 57 sauce

Saute bacon, cut into 1-inch pieces, in large skillet until partially cooked; then add onion and continue to cook until onion is tender. Remove bacon and onion. Drain drippings from skillet, reserving 2 Tbsp. drippings. Brown chicken pieces in drippings. Sprinkle lightly with salt and pepper. Drain excess fat; combine cooked bacon and onions with tomatoes, Heinz 57 sauce and sugar and add to chicken. Cover and simmer 45 minutes, basting occasionally. Thicken sauce if desired. Great with hot rice.

Greek Chicken

2 lbs. boned & skinned chicken breasts
1/4 tsp. garlic powder
1/4 tsp. oregano
1/4 cup lemon juice
1/4 cup margarine

1/2 cup olive oil
1/2 cup chopped onion
1 tsp. seasoned salt
1/8 tsp. salt

Combine garlic powder, olive oil, oregano, onion, lemon juice, seasoned salt, and salt. Marinate chicken breasts in mixture overnight. To cook, melt margarine in skillet. Saute until tender and evenly browned or bake for one hour at 350 degrees.

Yogurt-Baked Skinless Chicken

6 oz. vanilla yogurt
1 tsp. salt
2 tsp. Worcestershire sauce
1/2 tsp. paprika

1/4 tsp. Tabasco sauce
1/4 tsp. garlic powder
2-3 lbs. chicken, skinless and cut up
1 cup dry bread crumbs

Heat oven to 350 degrees. Use a 9x13 pan, greased with non-stick spray. Mix yogurt, salt, Worcestershire sauce, paprika, Tabasco sauce, and garlic powder. Dip chicken in mixture; roll in bread crumbs. Place chicken pieces in pan and bake uncovered one hour.

Pineapple Chicken

chicken pieces
1 cup pineapple juice
1 pkg. Hidden Valley Ranch dressing mix

1 tsp. seasoned salt
1 Tbsp. corn starch
1/8 cup water

Mix together pineapple juice, dressing mix, and seasoned salt. Marinate chicken pieces in sauce 2 to 24 hours. Drain sauce into saucepan. Bake chicken, skin side down, covered, for 45 minutes at 350 degrees. Mix together corn starch and water. Stir into marinade sauce and bring to boil. When thickened, turn chicken skin side up and spoon some of the sauce over chicken. Bake 15 minutes more, adding sauce another time.

Chicken A L'Orange

1/2 cup flour
1/2 tsp. salt
generous dash pepper
3 lbs. chicken, cut in pieces
1 Tbsp. oil

1 cup orange juice
2 Tbsp. packed brown sugar
2 tsp. soy sauce
1/2 tsp. ground ginger

Preheat oven to 350 degrees. Combine flour, salt and pepper; thoroughly coat chicken pieces with flour mixture. Heat oil in saucepan over medium heat; brown chicken and discard drippings. Combine orange juice, brown sugar, soy sauce and ginger. Put chicken in baking dish and pour sauce over chicken. Cover tightly and bake 35-40 minutes, until chicken is fork tender.

Delmarvelous Broiled Chicken

chicken pieces
cut lemon
melted butter
1 tsp. salt

1 tsp. sugar
1/4 tsp. paprika
1/8 tsp. pepper

Rub chicken pieces with cut lemon, squeezing to release juice. Coat with melted butter. Sprinkle with mixture of salt, sugar, paprika, and pepper (use half of mixture now). Broil 5 to 7 " from heat, skin side down. After 15 minutes, turn chicken over. Brush with melted butter and remaining salt and sugar mixture. Broil 35 to 50 minutes.

Country Style Chicken Kiev

2 to 3 lbs. chicken, cut in pieces
1/3 cup butter
1/4 cup fine dry bread crumbs
1 Tbsp. grated parmesan cheese
1/2 tsp. basil leaves
1/2 tsp. oregano leaves

1/4 tsp. garlic salt
1/8 tsp. salt
1/8 cup apple juice or white wine
1/8 cup chopped green onion
1/8 cup chopped fresh parsley

Heat oven to 375 degrees. Melt butter; combine bread crumbs, parmesan cheese, and seasonings. Dip chicken pieces in melted butter, then coat with crumb mixture. Reserve remaining butter. Place chicken skin side up in ungreased pan. Bake 50-60 minutes, until tender. Meanwhile, add to reserved butter: apple juice, onion and parsley. Heat with chicken or in separate pan 3-5 minutes until heated through. Serve sauce over chicken.

Crispy Parmesan Chicken

3 lbs. frying chicken, cut in pieces
1 egg, slightly beaten
2 Tbsp. milk
3/4 cup corn flake crumbs

1 1/2 tsp. salt
1/4 tsp. pepper
1/2 cup parmesan cheese

Combine corn flake crumbs (crushed corn flakes), salt, pepper and cheese; set aside. Wash and pat dry chicken pieces. Combine beaten egg, and milk. Dip chicken pieces in egg mixture, then roll in corn flake mixture. Place in well-greased baking pan, skin side up, and bake one hour at 350 degrees. Do not cover or turn chicken while baking.

Bacon & Mushroom Chicken

6 slices bacon
2 chickens, cut into pieces
1/2 cup flour
2 tsp. salt
1/4 tsp. pepper
2 cups chopped onion

garlic (or garlic powder)
1 can mushrooms
2 cans tomatoes
parsley
1 cup croutons

Fry the bacon until crisp; crumble and set aside. Wash and pat dry chicken pieces. Combine flour, salt and pepper. Coat each chicken piece with flour mixture, then brown in a little oil. Put in baking dish. Saute onion and garlic; stir in remaining flour mixture. Add liquid from canned mushrooms, along with tomatoes, and boil for 1 minute. Pour over chicken. Bake 1 hour at 350 degrees. Sprinkle croutons, bacon and mushrooms over chicken. Bake an additional 10 minutes.

Chicken Polynesian

1 or 2 chickens, cut into pieces
15 or 16 oz. can crushed pineapple

1 cup brown sugar
1/2 cup soy sauce

Brown chicken pieces in a little oil. Place in baking pan or Nesco roaster. Combine crushed pineapple, sugar and soy sauce and pour over chicken. Bake covered until done, about 1 1/2 to 2 hours at 350 degrees. Baste once or twice.

Great Fried Chicken

2 cups dry pancake mix
2 pkg. (0.9 oz.) Italian salad dressing mix
1 egg
1/3 cup plus 1 cup water
vegetable oil

3 lb. chicken, cut into pieces
1/4 cup cornstarch
10 oz. can chicken broth
2 chicken bouillon cubes
2-10 oz. cans beef gravy

Mix dry pancake mix with 1 pkg. salad dressing mix; set aside. Beat egg with 1/3 cup water; add remaining pkg. of salad dressing mix.   Coat evenly the chicken pieces in egg and water mixture first and then dry mixture. Set on paper toweling and let dry for about 10 minutes. Heat enough vegetable oil in skillet to give it a 1-inch depth, at 400 degrees. Fry 4 to 5 minutes on each side. Place in baking dish and bake at 350 degrees for 30 minutes. (For crispy chicken, bake uncovered; for moister chicken, cover with foil.) In a saucepan, combine 1 cup water and cornstarch. Blend until smooth. Add chicken broth, bouillon cubes and beef gravy to saucepan and cook over medium high heat. Cook and stir until thick and clear. Serve over chicken.

Microwaved Chicken Breast with Mushroom Sauce

3 Tbsp. butter or margarine
1 cup sliced fresh mushrooms
2 Tbsp. finely sliced green onions
1/3 cup milk
3 oz. cream cheese, cubed

1/4 tsp. chicken soup base
1/8 tsp. salt
1/8 tsp. white pepper
4 chicken breast halves or filets

In a glass baking dish, microwave 2 Tbsp. butter, mushrooms, and green onions for 3 to 4 minutes. Stir halfway through cooking time. Add milk, cream cheese, chicken soup base, salt and pepper. Cook 2 minutes. Stir until smooth, and cook 1 minute. Set aside. In another glass baking dish, microwave chicken breasts and remaining butter on HIGH for 6 to 8 minutes, or until meat is no longer pink. Spoon mushroom sauce over the chicken and cook 2 to 3 minutes. Makes 4 servings.

Microwave Chicken Breasts Italiano

3 to 4 oz. uncooked spaghetti noodles
3 cups cold water
1/4 tsp. salt
2 Tbsp. margarine
1/3 cup onion, finely chopped
6 chicken breast halves or filets
8 oz. tomato sauce
1/8 tsp. basil leaves

1/8 tsp. oregano leaves
1/8 tsp. salt
1/8 tsp. white pepper
1/4 cup whipping cream
1 Tbsp. parsley flakes
1/2 cup mozzarella cheese, shredded
1/4 cup stuffed green olives, sliced

Combine noodles, water and salt. Microwave on HIGH for 10-13 minutes, or until tender. Stir occasionally. Drain and set aside. In a 9x13 glass baking dish, combine margarine and onion. Microwave on HIGH for 3-4 minutes. Add chicken breasts to pan and cook 8-10 minutes, or until meat is no longer pink. In a bowl, combine tomato sauce, basil, oregano, salt, pepper, and whipping cream. Pour over chicken and cook 3-4 minutes. Sprinkle with parsley flakes, mozzarella cheese, and sliced green olives. Cook another 2-3 minutes. Serve over a small bed of spaghetti noodles. Makes 6 servings.

Chicken Breasts with Cheese Sauce

8-10 chicken breasts, deboned and skinned
1 onion, sliced thinly
3 cans cream of mushroom soup

1 lb. Velveeta cheese
green onions, chopped
2 oz. pimento, chopped

Lay chicken breasts in 9x13 baking dish. Salt and pepper to taste and place thin slices of onion over the chicken. Melt together the remaining ingredients and pour over chicken. Bake at 325 degrees for 1 hour, covered. Do not let it bubble; do slowly.

Lemon Chicken

4-6 boneless chicken breasts or thighs
1 tsp. vegetable oil
1 green onion, thinly sliced
1 egg, beaten
1/2 cup flour

pinch of rosemary & thyme
1/2 of a 3.5 oz. box of lemon pudding,
   regular, not instant
1 1/2 cups water

Preheat skillet over medium heat and add oil to heated pan. Dip meat in egg, then in flour to coat. Place meat carefully into pan and sprinkle on the onion, along with some herbs of your choice, if desired. Pan fry 3-4 minutes, turn over, and pan fry 2-3 minutes longer until golden brown. Whisk lemon pudding and water until blended. Pour into medium saucepan and cook over medium heat until boiling. Boil 1-2 minutes until smooth and clear. Remove from burner and spoon over chicken after it is on serving platter.

Creamy Chicken

4 boneless, skinless chicken breasts
1/2 cup chopped onion
5-6 fresh mushrooms, sliced
1/4 cup butter

1/4 cup white cooking wine or sherry
dash of Worcestershire sauce
1 pint cream (light or heavy)
salt and pepper

Lightly brown chicken in skillet; add onion, butter and mushrooms, and brown lightly. Add cooking wine and Worcestershire sauce and cook for two minutes. Add cream and salt and pepper to taste. Simmer on very low heat for 20-25 minutes until chicken is done. Too high of heat will curdle cream.

Hawaiian Chicken

8 pieces chicken
small jar apricot marmalade

1 pkg. dry onion doup mix
8 oz. bottle Russian salad dressing

Pat the chicken pieces dry and place in 9x13 baking pan. Cover the pieces with the apricot marmalade, then sprinkle on the soup mix and cover with the Russian salad dressing. Bake for 1 hour at 350 degrees.

Baked Chicken Italian Style

4 chicken breasts or thighs
15 oz. can tomato sauce
1 tsp. garlic powder

1/2 tsp. oregano
1 tsp. salt
1/4 tsp. pepper

Heat oven to 350 degrees. Wash chicken and dry on paper towels. Put tomato juice and spices in baking dish; mix until blended. Roll chicken in tomato juice, leaving chicken skin side down. Bake 1 hour at 350 degrees. Turn chicken over and bake for another 30 minutes or until tomato juice is absorbed by chicken.

Imperial Chicken

1 cup grated parmesan cheese
1 cup bread crumbs
1/2 cup fresh parsley, chopped
1 tsp. salt

1 tsp. pepper
8 halved chicken breasts, boned and skinned
1/2 cup margarine or butter
2 cloves garlic

Dip chicken in butter; roll in crumb mixture of remaining ingredients. Place in 9x13 pan. Bake at 350 degrees for 50-60 minutes.

Chicken Parisienne for Crock Pot or Nesco Roaster

6 medium chicken breast halves
salt
pepper
paprika
1/2 tsp. leaf rosemary (optional)

1/2 cup water
1 can cream of mushroom soup
1 can sliced mushrooms, drained
1 cup sour cream
1/4 cup flour

Sprinkle chicken breast lightly with the salt, pepper, paprika and rosemary. Place in 4-quart Nesco roaster or crock pot. Mix water, soup, sour cream and mushrooms; add flour and mix until well blended. Pour liquid over chicken. Cover and cook on low (225 degrees) for 6 to 8 hours. (You can cook on high for 2 1/2 to 3 hours, but then you should add the sour cream/flour mixture during the last 30 minutes.) Serve chicken and sauce over rice or noodles. Yield: 6 servings, 300 calories per serving.

Chicken Luncheon Loaf

3 lb. chicken, cooked and cut up
2 Tbsp. minced onion
2 oz. jar pimento, chopped
4 cups cubed stuffing bread (croutons)
2 cups cooked rice
2 well beaten eggs

1 cup evaporated milk
1 quart chicken broth
1 can cream of mushroom soup
1 can cream of chicken soup
2 Tbsp. lemon juice

Mix together the cut-up chicken, onion, pimento, stuffing bread, cooked rice, eggs, evaporated milk and chicken broth. Bake in 9x13-inch pan at 325 degrees for 1 hour. Cut into 12 to 15 squares. Mix together soups and lemon juice. Heat and pour over chicken loaf squares as served. Makes a great entree for a women's luncheon.

Chicken and Rice

1 chicken, cut in serving pieces
1 can cream of celery soup
1 soup can of milk

1 cup rice, uncooked
1 can cream of mushroom soup
1 pkg. dried onion soup mix

Butter a large baking dish or cake pan. Spread rice on bottom of pan; place cut-up chicken on rice. Mix soups, milk and dry onion soup mix. Pour over chicken. Cover with foil and bake at 250 degrees for 1 1/2 to 2 hours.

Chicken-Crouton Casserole

4 cups seasoned croutons
1 cup butter or margarine, melted
2 cans cream of celery soup
1 can milk

3 or 4 cups diced cooked chicken or turkey
10 oz. frozen peas
2 oz. jar pimentos, chopped
pepper to taste

Mix croutons and butter together and press half of mixture into a 9x13-inch pan. Mix remaining ingredients and pour over crouton mixture; top with remaining croutons. Bake at 350 degrees for 1 hour. Serves 12. Good way to use your leftover chicken or turkey.

Chicken Casserole

4 cups cooked, cut up chicken, seasoned
1-6.25 oz. pkg. white and wild rice, cooked
*   as directed , with seasoning packet*
1 cup chopped celery
4 oz, water chestnuts, sliced

2 cans cream of chicken soup
1 cup chopped green onion
1 cup green pepper (or less, if desired)
3/4 cup real mayonnaise

Mix soup and mayonnaise. Add remaining ingredients. Pour into 9x13 pan. Cover and refrigerate overnight. Bake at 325 degrees for 90 minutes.

Chickette

1 1/4 cup uncooked spaghetti, broken
*   into 2-inch pieces*
2 cups chicken or turkey, cut up
1/4 cup diced pimento
1/4 cup chopped green pepper
1 3/4 cup grated cheddar cheese

1/2 cup chopped onion
1 can cream of mushroom soup
1/2 cup chicken broth or water
1/2 tsp. salt
1/8 tsp. pepper

Cook spaghetti according to package directions and drain. Place chicken, pimento, green pepper and onion in 1 1/2 quart casserole. Pour in mushroom soup and chicken broth. Add salt, pepper, 1 1/4 cups cheese and spaghetti. With 2 forks, lightly toss until well mixed. Sprinkle remaining cheese on top. Chill. Bake at 350 degrees for 45 to 60 minutes.

Oriental Chicken Casserole

3 cups cooked chicken or turkey, diced
1 can mushrooms (4 oz.)
3 Tbsp. soy sauce
1/2 cup cashews or almonds

1 can cream of mushroom soup
1 cup celery, diced
1/2 tsp. onion, chopped
2 cups chow mein noodles

Put 1 cup noodles in bottom of ungreased casserole. Mix other ingredients and put on top of noodles. Cover with remaining noodles. Bake at 350 degrees for 45 minutes. Can be prepared ahead and last cup of noodles added before baking.

Apricot Glazed Chicken with Wild Rice

3-4 lbs. chicken pieces
12 oz. jar apricot preserves
2 Tbsp. red wine vinegar
1 tsp. salt

dash of pepper
1 pkg. long grain and wild rice
10 oz. frozen peas

Preheat oven to 400 degrees. Bake chicken pieces 30 minutes. Mix apricot preserves, vinegar, salt and pepper. Cook rice according to package directions. Add onion and chicken flavoring, if desired. After chicken has baked 30 minutes, spoon apricot mixture over chicken and bake 20 minutes more, basting occasionally. Stir frozen peas into cooked rice. Serve chicken pieces and extra sauce with rice pilaf.

Country Chicken and Potato Bake

3 medium potatoes, unpeeled, cut in cubes
1 medium onion, chopped
3 lbs. chicken pieces

1 tsp. salt
1 tsp. rosemary leaves, dried
1/4 tsp. pepper

Preheat oven to 425 degrees. Spray baking dish with non-stock spray. Mix all ingredients together in large bowl or plastic bag. Arrange in baking dish and bake one hour or until potatoes are done and juices run clear when chicken is pierced.

Chicken a la King Filling for Crepes

2 cups chicken, cooked and cubed
1/4 cup margarine, melted
1/3 cup flour
1 tsp. salt
1 cup chicken broth
1 cup milk

1/4 cup sliced mushrooms
2 Tbsp. pimento
1/2 cup frozen peas
1 Tbsp. minced onions
1/2 tsp. parsley
1/8 tsp. white pepper

Saute mushrooms and onions. In saucepan, combine margarine, flour and salt. Cook over medium heat, gradually adding chicken stock and milk, stirring constantly. Continue stirring until mixture thickens. Add remaining ingredients. Heat thoroughly. Spoon mixture on crepe, roll and garnish with sprig of parsley.

Grilled Shrimp

1 1/2 lbs. medium to large raw shrimp
salt and pepper to taste
2 Tbsp. olive oil
2 Tbsp. lemon juice

2 Tbsp. water
1 Tbsp. minced garlic
8 Tbsp. butter, melted
2 Tbsp. chives

Peel and devein shrimp. String on skewers, season to taste and brush with oil. Grill 4 inches from coals about 1 1/2 minutes per side. Mix together in saucepan the lemon juice, water, minced garlic, butter and chives. Heat through. Coat the shrimp with this glaze and serve.

Shrimp Stir Fry

2 small cans of peeled shrimp
　(or 1 lb. fresh shrimp, boiled and peeled)
1 green pepper, chopped
fresh tomatoes, cut up

fresh mushrooms, sliced
1 onion, chopped
1 can chicken broth
2 Tbsp. flour

Put all ingredients except broth and flour in a wok and cook on medium high heat for a few minutes. You can also add other vegetables such as pea pods, water chestnuts, bean sprouts, etc., if desired. Mix chicken broth and flour; add to stir fry and heat until it thickens. Serve over rice or noodles.

Chesapeake Bay Crabcakes

1 lb. fresh jumbo lump crabmeat
1/2 cup onions, finely chopped
1/2 cup celery, very finely chopped
5 Tbsp. butter
2 1/2 cups breadcrumbs
2 tsp. chopped parsley
1 tsp. dill, finely chopped
juice of 1/2 lemon

1/4 tsp. pepper
1/2 tsp. salt
2 small egg yolks
1 tsp. dry mustard (curry may be
   substituted)
2 tsp. heavy cream
2 cups flour
3/4 cup milk, lightly beaten with 1 egg

Place jumbo lump crabmeat in bowl. Saute onion and celery in 2 Tbsp. butter. When cool, add to crabmeat. Try not to break up lumps. Add parsley, dill, lemon juice, salt, pepper, and breadcrumbs. Blend egg yolks, mustard and cream. Add to crab mixture. Mix gently and refrigerate for 45 minutes. Shape gently into balls slightly smaller than tennis balls. Dip balls into flour, then into beaten egg and milk mixture. Gently flatten balls between two plates. Return to refrigerator for 50 minutes. Heat remaining butter in skillet, and carefully brown crab cakes for 4 minutes on each side. Makes 6 unbelieveable crab cakes, for a very special summer dinner with the flavor of the Bay in every bite! This recipe was given to me by Bette Ball.

Swedish Salmon Loaf

1 can red salmon
2 eggs
1 1/4 cups milk
3/4 cup cream
4 squares soda crackers, crushed
salt and pepper to taste

1 cup sugar
5 Tbsp. corn starch
2 cups boiling water
juice and grated rind of 1 1/2 lemons
3 egg yolks, slightly beaten

Clean salmon. Mix with other ingredients in first column above and pour into buttered loaf pan. Bake 1 hour at 350 degrees. Serve with the following sauce: Mix sugar and cornstarch. Add boiling water and cook in top of double boiler until clear. Add lemon juice and finely grated rind to cooked mixture. Mix 1 to 2 Tbsp. of hot mixture with yolks and return to mixture in double boiler. Cook until thickened, but do not boil. Serve sauce over each portion of salmon loaf. Delicious!

Tuna Pie

6 oz. can tuna, drained
1 cup shredded cheese, American or
    cheddar
3 oz. cream cheese, cut up
1/4 cup sliced green onions
2 oz. bottle pimento, chopped

2 cups milk
1 cup Bisquick baking mix
4 eggs
3/4 tsp. salt
dash nutmeg

Heat oven to 400 degrees. Grease pie plate. Mix tuna, cheeses, onion, and pimento in pie plate. Beat remaining ingredients 15 seconds in blender on high or 1 minute with hand beater. Pour into plate. Bake until knife inserted between center and edge comes out clean, 35 to 40 minutes. Cool 5 minutes. Serve with sliced tomatoes.

Tuna-Swiss Cheese Pie

1 9" pastry shell
12 to 13 oz. tuna, drained, flaked
1 cup shredded swiss cheese
1/2 cup chopped onion

3 eggs
1 cup real mayonnaise
1/2 cup milk

Pierce pastry shell with fork and bake in 375 degree oven for 10 minutes. In a large bowl, toss together the tuna, cheese and onion. Spoon into pastry shell. In bowl, stir together remaining ingredients. Slowly pour over tuna mixture. Bake 50 minutes at 375 degrees or until knife inserted in center comes out clean. Serves 8.

Tuna Chip Casserole

1 medium bag potato chips, crushed
2 - 6 oz. cans chunk tuna
1 can peas, drained

1 can cream of mushroom soup
1 1/2 cups milk

Grease casserole. Put in a layer of crushed potato chips, a layer of peas and a layer of tuna, using half of each. Pour 1/2 of heated soup-milk mixture over all. Repeat layers, ending with remaining soup-milk mixture and a few crushed potato chips on top. Bake at 350 degrees for 30 minutes.

Macaroni Tuna Hot Dish

7 oz. pkg. elbow macaroni, uncooked
2 cans cream of mushroom soup
1/2 soup can of water
2 - 13 oz. cans evaporated milk
4 hardboiled eggs, chopped

1/2 cup each onion, celery, green pepper,
    chopped
2 oz. pimento, chopped
1/2 lb. sharp cheddar cheese, cubed
2 - 6 oz. cans tuna

Mix together and refrigerate overnight. Bake at 350 degrees for 1 1/2 hours.

Creamed Tuna on Toast

2 cans cream of mushroom soup
2 soup cans of milk
1 large can tuna, drained
3 hard-boiled eggs, chopped

1 can peas or 1 1/2 cups frozen peas,
    thawed
salt and pepper to taste
buttered toast

Slowly add the milk to the soup in a 3-quart saucepan. When creamy, add the tuna, peas, and chopped eggs. Serve over buttered toast. Great for a lunch or quick supper.

Quiche

1 crust pie shell
1/2 lb. bacon, fried and crumbed
1 1/2 cups grated cheddar cheese
1 small onion, chopped and sauteed in
    1 Tbsp. bacon grease
3 eggs, well beaten

1 cup whipping cream
1/2 cup milk
1/2 tsp. salt
1/4 tsp. pepper
dash cayenne
1/4 tsp. dry mustard

Put fried bacon pieces, sauteed onion and cheese on crust. Mix remaining ingredients and pour over bacon and cheese. Bake at 375 degrees for 45 minutes.

Bacon Quiche

12 slices bacon, cooked and crumbled
1 cup shredded swiss cheese
1/3 cup onions, chopped
2 cups milk

1 cup Bisquick
4 eggs
1/4 tsp. salt
1/8 tsp. pepper

Preheat oven to 400 degrees. Lightly grease a 10-inch pie plate. Sprinkle bacon, cheese, and onions into pie plate. Beat milk, eggs, Bisquick and seasonings until smooth, about one minute. Pour into pie plate. Bake for 35 minutes or until top is golden brown and knife inserted halfway between center and edge comes out clean. Let stand 10 minutes before cutting.

Quiche Lorraine

6 eggs
one crust pie shell
1 cup ham slivers or
   8 slices bacon, crisp and crumbled
1 cup shredded Swiss cheese

1 cup half-and-half or light cream
1/2 tsp. salt
1/8 tsp. nutmeg
1/8 tsp. pepper

Beat eggs. Brush pie shell with small amount of beaten eggs. Prick bottom and sides with fork. Bake shell at 425 degrees (450 if metal pie plate) for about 5 minutes, until golden brown. Cool on wire rack. Sprinkle ham and Swiss cheese into pie plate. Beat cream and seasonings with eggs. Pour into pie plate. Bake in preheated oven (375 degrees for metal pan; 350 degrees for glass pie plate) until knife inserted halfway between center and outside edge comes out clean, about 35-40 minutes. Let stand 10 minutes before serving.

Monterey Cheese Puff

10 beaten eggs
1 tsp. baking powder
1/2 cup flour
1/2 tsp. salt
1/2 cup melted butter

2 cups small curd cottage cheese
1 lb. grated Monterey Jack cheese
1 cup onions, chopped
1 cup green peppers, chopped

Mix all together. Place in a 9x13-inch pan. Bake at 350 degrees for 30 minutes. Makes 12 or more pieces.

Breakfast for Six

8 slices bread, cubed & crust removed   4 cups milk
2/3 lb. Velveeta cheese, sliced   1 tsp. salt
8 eggs   1 tsp. mustard

Put bread cubes in 9x13" pan. Place cheese slices over bread. Beat together eggs, milk, salt and mustard and pour over bread and cheese. Cover and refrigerate overnight. Bake uncovered for one hour at 325 degrees. After 1/2 hour of baking, top with bacon bits, ham cubes, or 8 strips of bacon, fried and crumbled.

Breakfast Fondue

1 box croutons   3/4 tsp. dry mustard
2 cups shredded cheddar cheese   2 3/4 cups milk
2 lbs. link sausage, diced and fried   1 can cream of mushroom soup
6 eggs

Place croutons in greased 9x13 pan. Add cheese and meat. Beat eggs, mustard, 2 1/4 cups milk and pour over croutons, sausage and cheese. Refrigerate overnight. Before baking, pour soup and 1/2 cup milk over all. Bake at 350 degrees for 1 1/2 hours.

Fluffy Cheese and Egg Crepe Filling

4 eggs, scrambled   1/4 cup grated cheese, American, cheddar
1/2 lb. bacon, fried and crumbled   or Monterey Jack

Prepare 4 scrambled eggs. Spoon egg mixture onto crepe; sprinkle with crumbled bacon and grated cheese. Fold and place in baking dish. Top with additional cheese and place under broiler until cheese melts, approximately 2-3 minutes.

Susan's Kielbasa

1 lb. kielbasa, cut into 1/2 " pieces
3/4 cup sour cream
2 Tbsp. prepared brown mustard
1/4 tsp. salt

1 medium onion, sliced
4 cups thinly sliced cabbage
1/8 tsp. pepper

In large skillet combine kielbasa, onion, and cabbage. Cover and cook over medium heat 15-20 minutes, until cabbage and onion are soft and translucent. Stir in sour cream, mustard, salt and pepper. Heat through.

Reuben Sausage Casserole

3 medium potatoes, peeled and cubed
1 lb. ground sausage
1 pint can sauerkraut, drained

1/2 cup thousand island dressing
3 Tbsp. shredded fresh parsley
8 oz. shredded Swiss cheese

Partially boil potatoes in water and drain. Brown ground sausage in skillet. Put all ingredients together (except the cheese) and put in baking dish. Bake at 350 degrees for 30 minutes. The last 5 to 10 minutes, add the shredded Swiss cheese on top to melt.

Fantastic Pork Fajitas

1 lb. boneless pork loin
2 Tbsp. orange juice
2 Tbsp. vinegar
2 cloves minced garlic
1 tsp. oregano

1 tsp. cumin
1 tsp. seasoned salt
1 onion, sliced
1 green pepper, chopped

Cut pork loin into thin strips. Toss with orange juice, vinegar and seasonings. Stir fry in hot oil with onion and green pepper. Serve with warm tortillas.

Pork Sauce and Noodles

1/4 cup flour
1 Tbsp. curry powder
2 tsp. salt
1/4 tsp. pepper
3 lbs. lean pork shoulder,
   cut into 1 1/2 inch squares
2 Tbsp. butter or margarine
3 cups chicken bouillon

1 large onion, sliced
1 pound medium egg noodles, cooked
1 cup sliced celery
2 medium carrots, sliced
1 can (6 oz.) mushrooms, undrained
1 can (5 oz.) water chestnuts, drained and
   sliced
1/2 cup seedless raisins (optional)

Combine flour, curry powder, salt and pepper. Coat pork cubes with flour mixture; brown lightly in butter. Stir in bouillon and half the onion slices. Bring to boil. Reduce heat; cover and simmer 45 to 60 minutes or until meat is tender, stirring occasionally. Add remaining onion slices and other remaining ingredients, except noodles, to pork. Cover and cook about 15 minutes or until carrots are just tender. Serve with noodles. Makes 8 servings.

Annette Funicello's Peanut Butter Pork Chops

6 pork chops
1 medium onion, finely chopped
1 can cream of mushroom soup

1/2 cup peanut butter (Skippy, of course!)
2 cups water

Brown pork chops in oil. Remove from pan. Put peanut butter and soup in pan and heat, adding water gradually; stir until smooth. Add chops and onion; bring to boil. Reduce heat and simmer 50 minutes. Serve with rice.

"Chicken Lickin' Good" Pork Chops

6-8 pork chops
1/2 cup flour
1 1/2 tsp. salt
1 or 2 cans chicken and rice soup

1 1/2 tsp. dry mustard
1/2 tsp. garlic powder
2 Tbsp. oil

Mix together flour, mustard, salt and garlic powder. Coat pork chops lightly with flour mixture. Brown in oil in large skillet. Place browned pork chops in crock pot or Nesco 4-qt. roaster. Add soup. Cover and cook on low (250 degrees) 6-8 hours.

Baked Pork Chops with Potatoes

6 pork chops
salt and pepper
1/3 cup chopped onions
vegetable oil

4 cups thickly sliced potatoes
1 can cream of mushroom soup
1 1/4 cups milk

Rub pork chops on both sides with salt and pepper. Saute onions, plus the pork chops, in a little oil until chops are browned. Put potatoes in a 2-quart buttered baking dish. Arrange the browned pork chops over potatoes. To the cooked onions in the skillet, add soup amd milk. Stir and heat. Pour over chops in casserole. Bake, covered, for 30 minutes at 350 degrees. Uncover and bake 30-40 minutes more. Serves 6.

Pork Chops Provencale

4 pork chops
28 oz. can tomatoes, with liquid
1 cup whole mushrooms
1 large onion, cut in eighths
2 green peppers, chopped

1 clove garlic, minced
1/2 tsp. rosemary
1/2 tsp. oregano
salt and pepper to taste

Preheat oven to 375 degrees. In 5 or 6 qt. pan, over medium heat, brown pork chops in a little oil. Add remaining ingredients and bring to a boil. Cover and place in oven for 45 minutes. Remove from oven. Turn pork chops and stir the vegetables. Simmer, uncovered, on top of stove for 8-10 minutes. Serve with hot rice.

Pork Chops and Rice

2 cups rice (long grain), no Minute Rice
1 can cream of chicken soup
1 1/2 cups water

1 tsp. Mrs. Dash's seasoning or onion salt
4 to 6 pork chops

Take the 2 cups rice (not cooked) and put in greased cake pan. Mix together cream of chicken soup, water and Mrs. Dash's seasoning. Pour over rice and lay 4 to 6 pork chops on top of rice and soup mixture. Cover with foil. Bake at 325 degrees for 3 hours. If dry, pour a little water along the side (1/2 cup).

Pork Chops Stuffed

2 cans cream style corn
1 pkg. stuffing
1 can water chestnuts, sliced

1/4 cup onion, chopped
8 boneless pork chops
1/2 cup butter

Melt butter in 9x13" pan. Lay pork chops on butter. Mix corn, stuffing, onion and water chestnuts and arrange on top of meat. Cover with foil and bake at 300 degrees for 1 1/2 hours; uncover and continue to bake 1 more hour.

Pork Chops and Creamed Corn

4 boneless pork chops
1 small onion, chopped
1 large can of creamed corn
1/4 cup milk

3-4 large potatoes, boiled or baked
salt and pepper to taste
1 Tbsp. butter

Melt butter in skillet; brown pork chops in butter with the onion. Add the creamed corn and the milk into the skillet and let it simmer for 30 minutes. Serve with the potatoes.

Believe It Or Not Pork Chops

6 to 8 pork chops
1 cup ketchup

1 cup Coke

Brown pork chops and place in baking dish. Mix coke and ketchup together and pour over pork chops. Cover with foil. Bake at 375 degrees for 45 minutes. Believe it or not, this is surprisingly delicious!

Barbecued Pork Chops

2 1/2 cups water
1 Tbsp. sugar
2 tsp. black pepper
2 Tbsp. butter
1/4 cup vinegar
2 1/2 tsp. salt

2 Tbsp. worcestershire sauce
1/4 cup chopped onion
1 tsp. powdered mustard
2 tsp. chili powder
1/2 tsp. tabasco sauce
1 bud garlic

Brown chops. Combine all ingredients and pour over pork chops in a large baking dish. Bake at 325 degrees for 90 minutes. Turn chops after 45 minutes.

B-B-Q Ribs

1/4 cup brown sugar
1 1/2 tsp. salt
garlic
4 to 6 lbs. ribs
1 cup ketchup
1 onion, diced

1 tsp. paprika
1/2 tsp. dry mustard
2 Tbsp. Worcestershire sauce
1/2 cup vinegar
1 Tbsp. butter

Mix brown sugar, salt, paprika, mustard and garlic together and rub on ribs. Combine ketchup, Worcestershire sauce, vinegar, butter and onion and simmer for 4 to 5 minutes. Pour over ribs and bake 2 hours at 350 degrees.

Barbecued Ribs

4-6 lbs. lean pork ribs
2 large onions
1 tsp. garlic salt
1 1/2 Tbsp. salt
2 1/2 cup ketchup

4 1/2 Tbsp. brown sugar
4 1/2 Tbsp. vinegar
4 1/2 Tbsp. worcestershire sauce
1 1/2 Tbsp. prepared mustard
4 drops Tabasco pepper sauce

Trim fat off pork ribs. Cut into serving pieces and put into large kettle. Boil with onions, garlic salt and salt until well done, about 1 hour. Drain and cool. Combine remaining ingredients; dip ribs into sauce and bake in oven for 30-40 minutes at 350 degrees. Sauce can be prepared ahead and stored in a jar in the refrigerator until needed. Alternate cooking method: place ribs, onions, salt and garlic salt in baking pan and cook in oven at 250 degrees for 4 hours. Then pour sauce over meat and heat through, about 30 additional minutes.

Honey-Glazed Ham

1 ham
2 oranges, sliced
1/2 cup mustard
1/2 cup brown sugar

1/4 cup honey
2 Tbsp. orange juice
whole cloves

Score the top of ham after baking for 20 minutes. Insert orange slices and cloves. Mix remaining ingredients and pour glaze over ham. Continue to baste every 15-30 minutes with juices.

Country Ham Pie

1/2 tsp. dry mustard
2 tsp. water
3 Tbsp. butter or margarine
1 Tbsp. minced onion
3 Tbsp. flour
1 2/3 cups milk
3/4 cup diced celery

1/8 tsp. pepper
1/8 tsp. garlic powder
2 tsp. Worcestershire sauce
2 cups diced ham
1/2 cup frozen peas
Pastry for 1-crust pie
paprika

Mix mustard with the water and set aside about 10 minutes. Melt butter in saucepan, add onion and saute 2 minutes. Stir in flour, then add milk and celery. Bring to boil over medium heat and cook, stirring, until thickened, then simmer a few minutes. Stir in mustard, pepper, garlic powder and Worcestershire sauce. Add ham and peas. Turn into shallow 1 1/2 quart baking dish and cover with pastry. Bake in preheated 425 degree oven 25 minutes, or until pastry is lightly browned. Sprinkle with paprika. Makes 4 to 6 servings.

Green Bean and Ham Casserole

16 oz. frozen green beans, cooked
2 cups cooked rice
1/2 cup grated cheddar cheese
6 oz. can evaporated milk

1/4 cup water
2 cups chopped ham
1 can cream of mushroom soup
1/2 cup crushed corn flakes

Put all but corn flakes in greased casserole dish. Mix together. Top with corn flakes amd dot with 3 Tbsp. butter. Bake 40 minutes at 375 degrees. May also be used with broccoli instead of green beans.

Cheesy Broccoli Ham Bake

10 oz. pkg. chopped broccoli, thawed
1 cup cooked rice
10 oz. can cheddar cheese soup
6 oz. can "tender chunk" ham

1/2 cup sour cream
1/2 cup bread crumbs
1/3 cup butter, melted

Mix broccoli, rice, soup, ham and sour cream in a casserole dish and cover with buttered crumbs. Bake covered at 350 degrees for 30-35 minutes. Remove cover to brown bread crumbs.

Saucy Ham and Potato Bake

2 Tbsp. chopped onion
1/4 cup margarine
1/4 cup flour
1 tsp. salt
1/2 tsp. dry mustard
dash pepper

1 1/2 cups milk
2 cups shredded mild cheddar cheese
1/2 lb. ham, cut into 1/8" slices
6 cups cooked potato slices

Saute onion in margarine. Blend in flour and seasonings. Gradually add milk; cool, stirring constantly until thickened. Add 1 1/2 cups cheese; stir until melted. Toss potatoes in cheese sauce. Pour into 2-quart casserole, reserving 1 cup potato slices. Arrange ham and remaining potato slices on top of casserole. Bake at 350 degrees for 30 minutes. Top with remaining cheese.

Fried Rice

2 cups cooked rice, cold or day old
1/4 cup tiny shrimp
1/2 cup pork or ham, cut in strips
1/4 cup fresh green onion, chopped

1 fried egg, cut in small strips
3 Tbsp. oil
soy sauce

Cook pork in 1 Tbsp. oil until brown; add shrimp and cook together. Take out of pan and set aside. Crumble the rice and fry it with 2 Tbsp. oil; then add cooked meats. Put soy sauce on to taste. Add fried egg strips and green onion before serving. Easy to make in T-Fal wok.

GETTING MARRIED

My mother called and said, "Have I got a guy for you!" She had met him one Sunday night at church and proceeded to call me in Eau Claire, Wisconsin, to beg me to drive home the next weekend. I made the four hour drive home and sure enough, there he was in church - Mark Roe, fresh out of the Marine Corps, muscles everywhere! I left our conversation that night thinking, "Wow! I wonder what's going to happen now?" I later learned that Mark went to work the next day and told his co-workers that he had just met the girl he was going to marry. It was a match made in heaven because we met on February 14th, Valentines Day, 1982. We wrote letters back and forth, called on the phone, and eventually began making the long trip back and forth between Minnesota and Wisconsin to visit each other. The more I got to know Mark, the more I was impressed by his genuine compassion for others, his sensitivity, his gentlemanly manners, his kindness and humility, and it didn't hurt that he was also very handsome! We had grown up just 10 miles apart, but we had attended different high schools and did not meet until we were 23 years old.

We were engaged in October and married the following April 16, 1983. We had a fairytale wedding in Long Prairie, Minnesota, attended by almost 600 people (you have to invite almost everyone when you're from small towns.) My sisters organized the entire reception and everything went off without a hitch. The wedding was done in red, white and navy blue, because Mark had some Marine friends lined up to form a sword archway for us to walk under, with the Marines outfitted in "dress blues." Unfortunately, four days before the wedding, the Marines were shipped off to Japan. We recruited four brothers-in-law to dust off their navy blue suits to usher and we dropped the idea of the archway. The groomsmen wore navy blue tuxedoes and the bridesmaids wore red satin long skirts with white chiffon ruffled blouses.

After the wedding, Mark was so anxious to leave the church and get on with the honeymoon, that he forgot his suitcase and clothes. The next day my sister had to drive an hour to our hotel to bring his clothes, so we could leave for our honeymoon in the Florida Keys. We'll never let him forget that one!

Now, more than ten years later, we are still very happily married! For our tenth wedding anniversary, we celebrated by vacationing in Hawaii for ten days. What a wonderful time! We plan to grow old together, always making new memories.

Our Wedding Day

April 16, 1983

Breads

Waffles

1 1/4 cup buttermilk
1/2 tsp. salt
1 tsp. baking soda
1/4 cup sugar

1 1/2 cup flour
2 eggs, well beaten
4 Tbsp. melted shortening
1/2 tsp. vanilla

Sift together the salt, soda, sugar and flour; add to beaten eggs. Add buttermilk and beat; then add melted shortening and beat again. Add vanilla and mix. Makes 4 large waffles.

Deluxe Waffles

2 cups flour
3 tsp. baking powder
1 tsp. baking soda
3/4 tsp. salt

2 cups buttermilk or sour milk
4 eggs, well beaten
1/2 cup melted butter

Place dry ingredients in bowl. Combine buttermilk and eggs and add to flour mixture. Beat until smooth. Stir in melted butter.

Pancakes

2 eggs
1 1/2 cups milk
3 Tbsp. vegetable oil
1 1/2 cups flour

1 1/2 Tbsp. sugar
1 1/2 Tbsp. baking powder
3/4 tsp. salt

Beat the eggs. Add remaining ingredients and stir.

Yogurt Pancakes

1 cup plain yogurt
2 eggs, separated
3/4 cup flour
1 Tbsp. sugar

1 tsp. baking soda
1 tsp. salt
1/2 cup butter, melted

In large bowl, sift flour, baking soda and salt. In medium bowl, combine yogurt, sugar and egg yolks. Add to flour mixture. Stir in melted butter. Beat egg whites until foamy; fold into batter. Spoon onto greased griddle, and cook over medium heat, turning once until lightly browned on each side. (This recipe was given to me by Ashlea Ball Ebeling, Bette's daughter. She said her mother served these delicious pancakes on Sunday mornings and no one ever guessed they were made with yogurt!)

Ugnspannkaka (Swedish Oven Pancake)

2 or 3 egg yolks
1 quart milk
1/2 tsp. salt

2 tsp. sugar
flour to make consistency of thin dough

Mix ingredients well. Pour into well greased 9x13 pan. Bake at 475 degrees for 5 minutes. Reduce temperature to 350 degrees and bake 20 to 25 minutes longer. Strips of bacon or small pieces of salt pork may be placed on top of pancakes before baking.

Basic Crepe Recipe

1 1/2 cups milk
2 Tbsp. vegetable oil
3 eggs

1 1/2 cups flour
1/8 tsp. salt

Blender Method: Put all ingredients into blender container in order listed. Cover and process at high speed until smooth.
Electric Mixer Method: In a large mixer bowl, beat eggs well on medium speed. Gradually add dry ingredients alternately with milk and oil. Beat until smooth.
Note: Batter may be prepared just before using or held covered in the refrigerator until ready to use, up to 3 days. Just stir before using.
Yield: 20-24 crepes

Cornmeal Crepes

3/4 cup flour
1/2 cup cornmeal
pinch of salt

1 1/4 cup milk
3 eggs
1 Tbsp. margarine or butter, melted

Measure all ingredients into small mixing bowl. Beat with electric mixer at medium speed until ingredients are combined. It will be necessary to stir batter occasionally; cornmeal has a tendency to sink. Great with Taco Filling. Yield: 12 to 14 crepes

Whole Wheat Crepes

4 eggs
1 cup whole wheat flour
1/2 cup milk
1/2 cup water

1/2 tsp. salt
2 Tbsp. margarine or butter, melted
2 tsp. wheat germ

Measure all ingredients into large mixing bowl. Beat with electric mixer until all ingredients are combined. It will be necessary to stir batter occasionally; the wheat germ tends to sink. Great with Fluffy Cheese and Egg Crepe Filling. Yield: 12 to 14 crepes.

Good Sweet Muffins

1 egg
1/2 cup milk
1/4 cup vegetable oil
11/2 cups flour

1/2 cup sugar
2 tsp. baking powder
1/2 tsp. salt
1 cup blueberries (optional)

Heat oven to 400 degrees. Beat egg with fork. Add remaining ingredients, except blueberries, and stir until flour is moistened. Batter should be lumpy. Add blueberries, if desired. Fill muffin cups 2/3 full. Bake 20-25 minutes. Serve warm.

Bran Muffins

5 cups flour
3 cups sugar
5 tsp. soda
2 tsp. salt
15 oz. Raisin Bran cereal

1 cup oil
1 quart buttermilk
4 eggs
2 cups boiling water

Mix all together. Add Raisin Bran and boiling water last. Bake muffins at 400 degrees for 30 minutes. Makes approximately 5 dozen muffins. NOTE: This batter keeps in the refrigerator for about 1 month. Use only what you need each time you bake and have fresh muffins in the morning!

Apple Puff Muffins

2 cups Bisquick baking mix
1/4 cup sugar
1 tsp. cinnamon
1/2 cup applesauce

1/4 cup milk
1 egg
2 Tbsp. oil

Mix together the Bisquick, sugar, cinnamon and applesauce. Add remaining ingredients and mix together with spoon for 30 seconds. Drop into muffin tins. Bake 12 minutes at 400 degrees. When removed from oven, dip tops of muffins in melted butter and then in cinnamon sugar (1/3 cup sugar plus 1/2 tsp. cinnamon.) Makes 12 muffins.

Pumpkin Muffins

1 egg, beaten
1/2 cup canned pumpkin
1/2 cup milk
1 1/2 cups flour
1/2 cup white sugar
1/2 tsp. salt

2 tsp. baking powder
1/2 tsp. cinnamon
1/2 tsp. nutmeg
1/2 cup raisins
1/4 cup butter
1 Tbsp. brown sugar

Combine beaten egg with pumpkin and milk. In separate bowl, mix flour, baking powder, salt, white sugar, cinnamon and nutmeg. Add to pumpkin mixture. Cut in butter. Add raisins; mix gently. Fill greased or lined muffin tins 2/3 full. Sprinkle tops with brown sugar. Bake at 400 degrees for 18-20 minutes. Makes 12 small muffins. (This recipe is from Geneva Ball. Well worth all the measuring! Great as a mid-morning snack.)

Danish Puff

1 cup butter
2 cups flour

1 tsp. almond flavoring
3 eggs

Heat oven to 350 degrees. Cut 1/2 cup butter into 1 cup flour. Sprinkle with 2 Tbsp. water. Mix with fork. Round into ball. Divide in half. Pat into two strips, 12x3" on ungreased baking sheet. Mix 1/2 cup butter with 1 cup water; bring to boil. Remove from heat. Add almond flavoring. Beat in remaining 1 cup flour, stirring quickly to prevent lumps. Add eggs, 1 at a time, beating well after each addition until smooth. Divide in half and spread half over each strip of pastry. Bake 55-60 minutes. Frost with mixture of: 1/3 cup soft butter, 3 cups powdered sugar, 3 Tbsp. cream, 1 1/2 tsp. vanilla. Sprinkle with sliced almonds.

Delicious Danish Pastry

1 cup milk, scalded
1 cup margarine
1 pkg. dry yeast
3 Tbsp. sugar
3 lightly whipped egg yolks

1/4 tsp. salt
4 cups flour
1 beaten egg white
brown sugar
chopped nuts

Mix scalded milk with 1 cup margarine; heat until melted. When cool, stir in dry yeast, sugar, whipped egg yolks, salt and flour. Divide dough into 3 parts. Wrap each in plastic wrap and refrigerate until chilled thoroughly. For each part, roll out into rectangle on pastry cloth. Spread with softened butter or margarine, 1 beaten egg white, brown sugar and nuts. Fold dough lengthwise so that the sides overlap. Seal ends. Place on cookie sheet and let rise for 20 minutes. Bake at 425 degrees until golden brown, about 15 to 18 minutes. Cool slightly and frost with powdered sugar icing. Serve warm. Makes three large coffee cakes. Dough may be kept in refrigerator for a week.

Apple Danish Pastry

2 1/2 cups flour
1 tsp. salt
1 cup Crisco
1 egg yolk
milk to make 2/3 cup with egg yolk

10-12 apples, peeled and sliced
1 cup sugar
1 tsp. cinnamon
1 egg white

Mix together for crust: flour, salt, Crisco, egg yolk and milk. Roll out 1/2 crust to jelly-roll pan size. Add apples mixed with sugar and cinnamon. Top with another 1/2 dough. Beat egg white and brush on crust. Bake 350 degrees for one hour. Frost while warm with powdered sugar frosting. Serves 12-15 or more.

Swedish Kringla

2 cups flour
1 cup butter
1 Tbsp. plus 1 cup water

1/2 tsp. almond extract
3 eggs

Mix 1 cup flour, 1/2 cup butter and 1 Tbsp. water like pie crust and put on cookie sheet in two long strips 3 inches wide. Heat 1 cup water and 1/2 cup butter to boiling point, remove from heat and add1 cup flour immediately and stir until smooth. Add eggs, one at a time, and beat well after each addition. Add extract. Spread on strips of pastry. Bake at 350 degrees for 50-60 minutes. Cool. Frost with 1 cup powdered sugar, 1 Tbsp. butter and 1/2 tsp. almond extract. Add cream to spread easily. Put chopped almonds on top.

Kaffekaka (Swedish Coffee Cake)

1 pkg. cake yeast
5 Tbsp. sugar
3 cups flour
1 tsp. cardamom
1/2 cup butter
1 cup lukewarm cream
1/4 tsp. salt

1 egg
1/2 cup seedless raisins
1/2 cup chopped candied cherries
1 egg, slightly beaten
sugar
3 Tbsp. chopped almonds
candied cherry halves

Mix yeast with 1 Tbsp. sugar. Sift flour into large bowl, add cardamom, dot with butter. Add cream, yeast mixture, remaining sugar, salt, egg, raisins and cherries. Beat until smooth and firm. Place in well-buttered baking dish, cover and allow to rise. Brush lightly with beaten egg. Sprinkle with sugar and chopped almonds, and a few halved candied cherries. Bake at 325 degrees for 20 minutes.

Streusel Filled Coffee Cake

3/4 cup sugar
1/4 cup shortening
1 egg
1/2 cup milk
1 1/2 cups + 2 Tbsp. flour
2 tsp. baking powder

1/2 tsp. salt
1/2 cup brown sugar
2 tsp. cinnamon
2 Tbsp. butter, melted
1/2 cup chopped nuts

Heat oven to 375 degrees. Mix shortening with sugar and egg; mix thoroughly. Stir in milk. Combine 1 1/2 cups flour, baking powder and salt; stir into creamed mixture. Spread half of batter in greased and floured 9-inch pan. Combine brown sugar, 2 Tbsp. flour, cinnamon, melted butter and chopped nuts. Sprinkle half of this streusel mixture over batter in pan. Add remaining batter; then remaining streusel mixture on top. Bake for 25 to 35 minutes. Note: Blueberries may be used instead of streusel mixture.

Blueberry Coffee Cake

1 pkg. or box blueberry muffin mix
2 Tbsp. cooking oil
1 egg

1/2 cup water
1/3 cup brown sugar
1 tsp. cinnamon

Preheat oven to 350 degrees. Empty blueberries into strainer; wash under cold running water and set aside to drain. Pour oil into one 8 or 9-inch square or round pan. Tilt pan to cover bottom with oil. Put muffin mix, egg and water into pan. Stir with fork until blended, about 1 minute. Sprinkle drained blueberries, brown sugar and cinnamon over batter. Use a fork to fold into batter just enough to create a marbled effect. Scrape sides and spread batter evenly in pan. Bake at 350 degrees for 25 to 35 minutes, until coffee cake tests done with a toothpick. Use a knife to loosen cake from sides. Cut and serve directly from pan.

Holiday Coffee Cake

1 cake mix (spice, caramel or yellow)
1 cup chopped nuts
1/2 cup sugar

1 tsp. cinnamon
1/2 cup butter or margarine, melted

Prepare cake mix according to package directions. Pour into a 9x13-inch cake pan. After 15 minutes in the oven at the temperature stated on box, remove cake and sprinkle on a mixture of the chopped nuts, sugar, and cinnamon. Then pour melted butter over all. Continue baking until done, 15 to 20 minutes. Serve warm. May be frozen for future enjoyment!

Pull-Apart Caramel Rolls

2 loaves frozen bread dough
3 tsp. cinnamon
1/2 cup melted butter
1 cup brown sugar

1 pkg. vanilla pudding (large box, not
instant)
3 tsp. milk

Thaw frozen bread dough. Grease 9x13 pan. Tear 1 loaf bread dough into pieces. Place in pan. Sprinkle cinnamon over pieces. Mix together butter, brown sugar, pudding mix and milk. Pour over pieces of bread dough. Tear second loaf of dough and put on top of first loaf. Try to fill in empty spots. Let rise four hours. Bake at 350 degrees for 30 minutes. Cool 15 minutes (very important.) Flip over onto cookie sheet.

Butterscotch Rolls

1/2 cup margarine, melted
maraschino cherries, sliced
1/2 cup nuts
2 loaves frozen bread dough, thawed

6 oz. butterscotch pudding mix, not
instant
1/2 cup brown sugar
1/2 tsp. cinnamon

Grease bundt pan; put in cherries and sprinkle with 1/2 of the nuts. Cut one loaf of bread dough into 24 pieces. Place in pan. Combine pudding mix, brown sugar and cinnamon; sprinkle over the bread in the pan. Drizzle the melted margarine over this and sprinkle remaining nuts on top. Cut remaining loaf of bread dough into 24 pieces and put into bundt pan. Cover; let rise until double in size. Bake at 350 degrees for 30 minutes. When done, let cool 5 minutes; invert onto waxed paper.

Orange Butter Coffee Cake Rolls

1 pkg. yeast
1/4 cup warm water
1 cup sugar
1 tsp. salt
1/2 cup dairy sour cream

1/2 cup butter
2 3/4 cups flour
1 cup coconut, toasted
2 Tbsp. grated orange rind
2 eggs

Dissolve yeast in warm water. Combine 1/4 cup sugar, salt, eggs, sour cream and 6 Tbsp. butter; add yeast. Gradually add flour to form stiff dough, beating well. Let rise until doubled. Combine 3/4 cup sugar, coconut and orange rind. Knead dough about 15 times; roll half of dough into a 12-inch circle. Brush with 1 Tbsp. butter. Sprinkle with 1/2 of coconut mixture. Cut into 12 wedges and roll, starting at wide edge like crescent rolls. Place rolls, point side down, in 3 rows in greased 9x13" pan. Do the same with rest of dough. Let rise until light. Bake at 350 degrees until golden brown, about 15 to 20 minutes. Leave in pan and top with powdered sugar glaze. Sprinkle with coconut.

Easy Caramel Orange Ring

1 Tbsp. butter, softened
1/2 cup orange marmalade
2 Tbsp. chopped nuts
1 cup firmly packed brown sugar

1/2 tsp. cinnamon
2-10 oz cans refrigerated buttermilk,
    flaky biscuits
1/2 cup butter, melted

Grease bundt pan with 1 Tbsp. butter. Place teaspoonfuls of orange marmalade in pan. Sprinkle with nuts. In a small bowl, combine brown sugar and cinnamon. Mix well; set aside. Dip individual biscuits in melted butter, then sugar mixture. Stand biscuits on edge in pan, spacing evenly. Sprinkle with remaining sugar mixture and drizzle with remaining butter. Bake near center of 350 degree oven for 30-40 minutes. Cool upright in pan for 5 minutes; invert onto serving plate.

Swedish Cinnamon Rolls with Cardamom

2 cups milk, scalded
3/4 cup shortening
3/4 cup sugar
1/2 cup lukewarm milk
2 eggs, beaten
1 pkg. cake yeast

2 tsp. salt
6-7 cups flour
1 1/2 dozen cardamom pots, shelled and
  crushed fine
softened butter
cinnamon and sugar mixture

Melt shortening in scalded milk; stir in sugar while cooling. Dissolve yeast in lukewarm milk. Add yeast mixture to milk. Add eggs, salt and flour combined with cardamom. Knead. Turn dough into a greased bowl and let rise. When double in bulk, punch down, let rise again. Divide dough into 3 parts. Roll each part as thin as possible into a 9x18-inch oblong pan. Spread with softened butter, sprinkle with sugar-cinnamon mixture. Roll up and cut each into 1 1/2 inch slices. Dip each in melted butter, then in sugar-cinnamon mixture. Place in greased 9x13 pans. Let rise; bake at 450 degrees for 10 minutes. Lower temperature to 350 degrees and bake another 20 minutes. Makes 3 dozen rolls.

Grandma Ruby's Swedish Doughnuts

1 1/4 cups sugar
2 whole eggs
2 egg yolks
4 Tbsp. whipping cream
3/4 cup milk
4 cups flour

1/2 tsp. salt
6 tsp. baking powder
1 1/4 tsp. nutmeg
1 1/4 tsp. lemon extract
2 Tbsp. butter, melted

Mix sugar, eggs, yolks, cream and milk with mixer until well blended. Add dry ingredients and mix with wooden spoon until smooth. Add rest of ingredients and mix well. Chill dough one hour. Roll out on floured board and cut with doughnut cutter. Fry in lard at 375 degrees. Dough may be put through doughnut maker, in which case do not chill.

Rolls (from frozen bread dough)

Thaw bread dough. Spread out to form a rectangle. Spread lots of butter, cinnamon and sugar over the dough. Roll up; cut in one-inch rolls. Place in greased pan and let rise. Bake at 350 degrees for 30 minutes.

Popovers

1 1/4 cup milk
1 1/4 cup flour

1/2 tsp. salt
3 eggs

Preheat oven to 450 degrees. Generously grease popover cups. Pour milk into medium sized mixing bowl. Add flour and salt. With rotary beater or wire whisk beat until well blended. Do not overbeat. One at a time add the eggs, beating just until completely blended after each addition. Pour batter into popover cups, filling three-fourths full. Do not scrape bowl. Bake at 450 degrees for 20 minutes. Reduce oven temperature to 350 degrees and continue baking 15-20 minutes or until golden brown. Serve immediately. Recipe makes 6 servings.

Diane's Rolls

1/4 cup shortening
1 cup scalded milk
1 small pkg. dry yeast
1/4 cup warm water

3 1/2 cups flour
1/4 cup sugar
1 egg

Melt shortening into scalded milk. Mix yeast with warm water. Mix flour and sugar; add milk and shortening to flour mix. Add egg, then yeast and water. Put into warm bowl, greased with butter. Cover and chill for 2 hours or until it rises. Take dough out and roll out. Put some butter on top. Pull apart and put in little balls on greased baking sheet. Let rise 1 hour more. Bake at 400 degrees for 12-15 minutes.

Overnight Rolls

3 cups lukewarm water
1/2 pkg. yeast
1 cup sugar
1/2 cup melted lard

1 tsp. salt
2 eggs, beaten
10 cups flour

Combine water, yeast and sugar; stir until dissolved. Add remaining ingredients. Use 1/2 cup flour to knead bread. Start at 5 PM. Punch down every hour until 11 PM. Put in pans as rolls. Bake at 375 degrees in morning until golden brown, about 15 minutes to 20 minutes.

Angel Biscuits

2 1/2 cups flour
1 tsp. baking powder
1 tsp. salt
1/8 cup sugar

1/2 cup solid shortening (like Crisco)
1 pkg. dry yeast
1/4 cup warm water
1 cup buttermilk

Dissolve yeast in warm water. Mix dry ingredients. Cut in solid shortening. Stir in buttermilk and yeast. Refrigerate or roll out on a floured cloth and cut with a biscuit cutter. Bake 10-12 minutes in a 400 degree oven, on a greased cookie sheet.

Cheese Bread

1/2 cup margarine, melted
1/2 bottle Italian dressing

1 loaf French bread
grated mozzarella cheese

Combine melted margarine and dressing. Cut French bread in half the long way. Pour dressing mixture over bread; top with grated mozzarella cheese. Bake at 350 degrees for about 15 minutes. Slice into serving portions.

Garlic Toast

large loaf French bread
1 lb. butter

2 Tbsp. Schilling Garlic Bread Sprinkle
Schilling Salad Supreme

Slice French bread into thin (1/4" to 1/2") slices. Soften butter and add Schilling Garlic Bread Sprinkle. Generously butter one side of bread and place on cookie sheet. Sprinkle with Schilling Salad Supreme and bake in 275 degree oven for 45 minutes. Cool. Freezes very well.

Wheat Bread

1 pkg. Red Star yeast
1/2 cup lukewarm water
2 tsp. sugar
2 cups water
3 Tbsp. molasses

1/2 cup sugar
1 heaping Tbsp. salt
1/2 cup wheat bran (heaping)
1/2 cup solid shortening
flour

Mix lukewarm water and 2 tsp. sugar in a cup. Add yeast and let rise in cup until it comes to the top. In another pan, put 2 cups water, molasses, 1/2 cup sugar, salt, wheat bran and solid shortening. Add yeast and mix. Add flour until it kneads nicely. Let rise until double in size. Grease bread pans. Knead dough into loaves and then grease the loaves with shortening. Put in pans and let rise until double in size. Bake at 350 degrees for 45 minutes.

Swedish Rye Bread

2 cups water
1/2 cup brown sugar
1 tsp. salt
1 tsp. caraway seed
1 tsp. anise

1 Tbsp. shortening
1 pkg. yeast
3 1/2 cups white flour
2 cups rye flour

Combine water, sugar, salt, caraway seed, anise and shortening and cook 3 minutes. Cool to lukewarm. Add yeast and white flour; mix to a soft dough. Let rise about 1 1/2 hours. Add rye flour to make a stiff dough; knead lightly. Place in greased bowl; cover with damp cloth. Let rise until doubled, about 2 hours. Knead; divide in 3 portions. Cover and let rest 10-15 minutes. Mold into loaves; place in greased pans. Cover and let rise until double. Bake in 375-400 degree oven 35-45 minutes.

Poppy Seed Bread

3 cups flour
1 1/2 tsp. salt
1/2 tsp. baking powder
2 1/2 cups sugar
1 1/2 cup milk

1 1/8 cup vegetable oil
1 1/2 Tbsp. whole dry poppy seed
3 eggs
1 1/2 tsp. vanilla
1 1/2 tsp. almond flavoring

Stir together the flour, salt, baking powder and sugar. Add remaining ingredients; beat for 2 minutes. Grease 2 loaf pans. Pour batter into pans. Bake 1 hour and 15 minutes at 350 degrees. Meanwhile, mix together 3/4 cup sugar, 1/4 cup orange juice, 1/2 tsp. vanilla, 1/2 tsp. almond flavoring and 2 tsp. butter. Simmer until sugar dissolves. Pour over bread immediately when you take it out of the oven.

Cherry Nut Bread

1 cup white sugar
1/2 cup butter
2 eggs
2 1/2 cups flour
2 tsp. baking powder
1/4 tsp. salt

1/2 cup milk
1/2 cup cherry juice
1 tsp. vanilla
16 maraschino cherries, finely cut up
1/2 cup chopped walnuts

Cream shortening and sugar. Add eggs and beat. Add remaining ingredients. Put into greased and floured loaf pan; bake at 325 degrees for 1 hour.

Mom's Banana Bread

1/2 cup shortening
1 tsp. vanilla
1 1/3 cups brown sugar, packed
2 eggs
2 cups flour

1 tsp. baking soda
1/4 tsp. salt
1/4 cup sour milk
1 cup mashed bananas
1/2 cup chopped nuts

Cream together the shortening, vanilla and sugar. Add eggs and beat thoroughly. Stir in dry ingredients alternately with sour milk and mashed bananas. (To make sour milk, add 1 Tbsp. vinegar or lemon juice to milk to make 1 cup.) Mix until smooth. Stir in nuts. Bake in greased 5x9-inch loaf pan or two 3x7-inch pans. Bake 50-60 minutes at 350 degrees.

Zucchini Bread

3 eggs
1 cup vegetable oil
2 1/2 cups sugar
2-3 cups zuchini, peeled and grated
3 tsp. vanilla
3 cups flour
1 tsp. baking soda
1 tsp. salt

1 tsp. baking powder
3 tsp. cinnamon
1 1/2 tsp. nutmeg
dash of ginger
dash of ground cloves
1 cup chopped nuts
1 1/2 cups raisins

Beat eggs; add oil, sugar, and vanilla. Mix well and add zuchini. Combine dry ingredients and mix with zuchini mixture, blending thoroughly. Add nuts and raisins and blend. Pour into greased and floured loaf pan and bake at 350 degrees for 1 hour.

Pumpkin Bread

1 1/2 cups sugar
2 eggs
1 3/4 cups flour
1 tsp. soda
1/2 tsp. cloves
1/2 tsp. nutmeg
1/3 cup water
1/2 cup chopped nuts

1/2 cup vegetable oil
1 cup pumpkin
1/4 tsp. baking powder
1 tsp. salt
1/2 tsp. cinnamon
1/4 tsp. allspice
1/2 cup raisins (optional)

Add sugar to oil and then add eggs and pumpkin. Blend spices with flour; add flour mixture, water , nuts and raisins to pumpkin mixture; mix well. Pour into two small or one large greased loaf pan(s). Bake at 350 degrees for 1 hour. Very Good!

ERIC

"It's a boy?" That was Mark's first statement as I gave birth to our first child. My doctor had been telling us she thought it was a girl, so we were expecting to greet "Erica." We were so surprised when "he" was born, but so pleased and relieved that he was healthy and had all the necessary parts! Eric was small at birth, 6 lb., 14 oz., because he was born three weeks early. I finished work at CVN about 9 PM on Wednesday evening and at 6 AM Thursday  morning, contractions had started. Eric was born at 4 PM that afternoon, October 15, 1987, with no complications, thank God.

There's nothing so special and so scary as having that first newborn home - so many questions, so few answers. Eric has been such a blessing to us. He's a lot like his daddy in that he's very inquisitive about how things work, what's inside certain things, how to build things, etc. He also has a shyness about him and a very sensitive heart. He's concerned that everyone is happy, and his feelings get hurt easily. I love his sensitive heart; it moves him to want to do kind things. He often brings Mark and me breakfast in bed. Breakfast consists of a 9x13-inch cake pan with a slice of bread in it with peanut butter an inch thick, a banana, peeled and already brown, leftover carrots from the night before or whatever else he can find in the refrigerator. I don't know whether to laugh or cry tears of joy because he's so sweet.

I am having to get used to all the reptiles that come through our home. We've had three turtles, several frogs, five different chameleons, and now a ribbon snake and a corn snake, both of which are harmless and about as big around as my pinky finger. They stay in an aquarium with a wire mesh lid so that I can sleep peacefully at night!

Eric is in kindergarten and it seems that he really likes school. He is very smart and very creative with his imagination. I'm already so proud of him and we've only just begun!

Eric

Mark is such a good daddy to both of the boys.

Pastries & Desserts

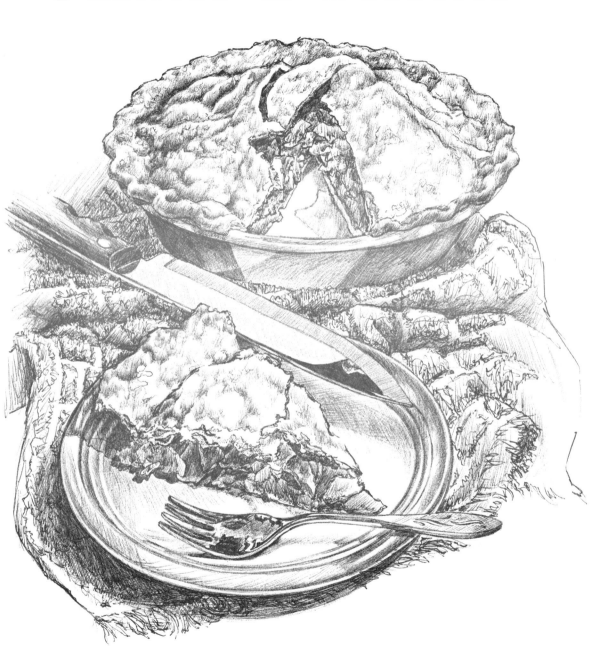

Butter Brickle Dessert

1 lb. crushed Hydrox cookies (or Oreos)
1 cup margarine
6 oz. chocolate chips
1 1/2 cups evaporated milk

2 cups powdered sugar
1 tsp. vanilla
1/2 gallon butter brickle ice cream
chopped nuts

Combine 1/2 cup melted margarine and the crushed cookies; pat into 9x13-inch pan and refrigerate 1 hour. Combine remaining 1/2 cup margarine, chocolate chips, evaporated milk and powdered sugar. Heat to boiling; boil 8 minutes, stirring constantly. Remove from heat and add vanilla. Cool, stirring occasionally. Meanwhile, put ice cream over crust. Freeze. When chocolate sauce is cooled, pour over ice cream. Top with chopped nuts. Keep in freezer.

Ice Cream Bombe

1/2 gallon vanilla ice cream
1/2 gallon chocolate ice cream
2 cups heavy cream
1/4 cup sugar

2 tsp. vanilla
1 box chocolate covered mint patties
1/2 cup walnut pieces

Spread vanilla ice cream in a large flat pan, like a broiler pan. Top with chocolate ice cream. (Have ice cream softened a bit first and cut in slices to place in pan.) Place in freezer while you whip the heavy cream with the sugar and vanilla. Chop the mint patties (green centers are prettiest) and walnuts. Fold into whipped cream and spread over ice cream. Freeze and cut into squares to serve.

Easy Frozen Dessert

1/2 cup margarine, melted
1/2 cup brown sugar
3 cups Rice Krispies

1 cup coconut
1/2 cup chopped nuts
1/2 gallon (or less) ice cream, any flavor

Blend melted margarine and brown sugar. Add Rice Krispies, coconut and chopped nuts. Put 1/2 of mixture into the bottom of a 9x13 pan. Spread ice cream over bottom layer. Top with remaining mixture. Freeze.

Calypso Dessert

1 box chocolate wafers, crushed
1/4 cup butter or margarine, melted
1/2 gallon vanilla ice cream
4 oz. German chocolate
1/4 cup butter

2/3 cup sugar
1/8 tsp. salt
2/3 cup evaporated milk
1 tsp. vanilla

Combine chocolate wafer crumbs and 1/4 cup melted butter; mix and spread in 9x13-inch pan. Chill until hard. Put ice cream over wafers and freeze until hard. Boil German chocolate, butter, sugar, salt and evaporated milk; boil 4 minutes. Add vanilla. Pour over ice cream and freeze again.

Chocolate Peppermint Dessert

1 1/4 cups butter or margarine
3 cups graham cracker crumbs
2 cups powdered sugar
1 tsp. vanilla
dash of salt

2 squares chocolate, melted
3 eggs, separated
chopped nuts
1/2 gallon peppermint ice cream

Melt 1/2 cup butter or margarine; stir in graham cracker crumbs. Put in 9x13-inch pan. Bake 8-10 minutes at 375 degrees. Cool. Mix remaining butter, sugar, vanilla, salt, chocolate, egg yolks and nuts. Beat egg whites until stiff. Fold into chocolate mixture. Pour over crust. Chill. Soften ice cream slightly and spread over chocolate layer. Garnish with crumbs. Freeze until ready to serve. Let stand at room temperature for 30 minutes before serving.

Peach Delight

6 oz. pkg. peach jello
2 cups hot water
2 cups cold water
1 No. 2 can crushed pineapple,
    drain and save 1/2 cup juice
1 cup miniature marshmallows
2 bananas, diced

1/2 cup chopped nuts
1 whole egg
1/2 cup sugar
2 tsp. butter
2 tsp. flour
3 oz. cream cheese
8 oz. Cool Whip

Prepare jello as directed and mix with drained pineapple, marshamallows, bananas and nuts. Pour into 9x13 pan and refrigerate. Melt butter in small saucepan (medium heat) and add flour. When smooth, add pineapple juice, sugar and egg. Stir until thick, using wire whip. Remove from heat; add cream cheese while warm. When cooled, fold in Cool Whip. Spread this mixture on top of the jello mixture and refrigerate at least 4 hours (overnight worksbest).

Easy Peach Cobbler

1/2 cup margarine
1 cup self-rising flour
1 cup sugar

1 cup milk
1 tsp. vanilla
1 large can sliced peaches, with juice

Place margarine in a deep ovenproof bowl or casserole and place in a 450 degree oven to melt while assembling the other ingredients. Mix together the flour, sugar, milk and vanilla. Stir until smooth. Remove the bowl from the oven and pour flour mixture over the melted margarine. Don't stir. Pour can of peaches over the top of this. Again, don't stir. Return to the oven and cook at 450 degrees for 10 minutes. Turn oven to 375 degrees and cook until crust comes to the top and is golden brown.

Pineapple Delight Dessert

4 eggs, separated
1 cup sugar
1 cup crushed pineapple

3 oz. pkg. lemon jello
24 vanilla wafers
4 Tbsp. butter, melted

Crush the wafers (graham crackers may be substituted) and mix with melted butter. Press crumb mixture into bottom of 9x13" pan, saving a few crumbs for top. Put pan in freezer or refrigerator. Cook egg yolks, crushed pineapple and 1/2 cup sugar in double boiler until thick. Add jello and cool. Beat the 4 egg whites until stiff; add the remaining 1/2 cup sugar and fold into the pineapple mixture. Pour over prepared crust. Sprinkle with a few crumbs. Let stand overnight in the refrigerator.

Banana Split Dessert

2 cups graham cracker crumbs
1/2 cup melted butter
2 cups powdered sugar
1 cup soft butter
1 tsp. vanilla
2 eggs

3 bananas, sliced
1 cup strawberries, sliced
1 can crushed pineapple, drained
3 cups whipped cream
1 cup crushed nuts
chocolate sauce & cherries

Combine graham cracker crumbs and melted butter. Press into 9x13" pan. Combine powdered sugar, soft butter, vanilla and eggs. Beat for two minutes. Pour over prepared crust. Top filling with sliced bananas, then sliced strawberries and lastly the pineapple. Frost with whipped cream and top with crushed nuts. Refrigerate at least 12 hours. Serve with chocolate sauce and cherry, if desired.

Apple Crisp

20 oz. can Comstock sliced apples,
    well drained
3/4 cup brown sugar, packed
1/2 cup flour

1/2 cup uncooked rolled oats
3/4 tsp. cinnamon
3/4 tsp. nutmeg
1/3 cup butter or margarine, softened

Heat oven to 375 degrees or you can use the 4 or 6-quart Nesco roaster. Spray baking pan or Nesco pan with Pam or other non-stick spray. Spread apple slices in pan. Mix remaining ingredients thoroughly; sprinkle over apples. Bake until topping is golden brown, about 30 minutes. Serve warm.

Cranberry Dessert

1 pkg. cranberries, chopped
1 cup sugar
12 oz. Cool Whip

1 pkg. miniature marshmallows
1 cup crushed pineapple

Combine chopped cranberries and sugar. Let stand several hours or overnight. To this mixture, add remaining ingredients. Chill. Really Good!

Rhubarb Crunch

11/4 cups flour
5 Tbsp. powdered sugar
1/2 cup butter
2 eggs, beaten

1 1/2 cups white sugar
3/4 tsp. baking powder
pinch salt
3 cups unsweetened rhubarb

Combine 1 cup flour with powdered sugar and butter. Mix as pie crust and pat into 8x8-inch pan. Bake 15 minutes at 350 degrees. Combine beaten eggs, white sugar and 1/4 cup flour; add baking powder and salt. Mix in rhubarb and pour over crust. Bake at 350 degrees for 35-40 minutes.

Rhubarb Dessert

1 Pillsbury Plus yellow cake mix
4 cups chopped rhubarb
3 oz. pkg. strawberry jello

1 cup flour
1 cup sugar
1/2 cup margarine

Grease a 9x13-inch pan. Spread dry cake mix in pan. Add rhubarb and sprinkle dry jello over rhubarb. Blend flour, sugar and butter until crumbly. Sprinkle over top. Bake 30-35 minutes at 350 degrees. Serve with whipped cream.

Cherry Angel Dessert

1 angel food cake, cut into 1/2-inch cubes
1 can cherry pie filling
1 pkg. instant vanilla pudding mix

1 1/2 cups milk
1 cup sour cream
Cool Whip or whipped cream

Place half of the angel food cubes into a 9-inch square pan. Spoon cherry pie filling over cake. Top with remaining angel food cubes. In a bowl, combine pudding mix, milk and sour cream; beat until smooth. Spoon over cake. Chill at least 5 hours. Tastes great when topped with Cool Whip or whipped cream. Serves 9.

Strawberry Dessert

1/2 lb. butter
2 1/2 cups powdered sugar
1 quart strawberries, sliced & sweetened

1 cup whipping cream, whipped
2 eggs, beaten
8 oz. vanilla wafers, crushed

Put half of the crushed vanilla wafers in the bottom of a 9x13 pan. Cream butter and sugar together; add eggs and beat well. Spread mixture on wafers. Next spread strawberries over the top. Spread whipped cream next and top with remaining crushed vanilla wafers. Refrigerate 24 hours before serving.

Strawberry Marshmallow Dessert

1 cup flour
1/2 cup butter, softened
1/4 cup brown sugar
1/2 cup nuts
24 marshmallows

2/3 cup milk
1/2 pint whipping cream, whipped
3 oz. box strawberry jello
1 cup boiling water
2 cups frozen, sweetened strawberries

Combine flour, softened butter, brown sugar and nuts. Mix and press into greased 9x13 pan. Bake at 325 degrees for 15 minutes. Cool. Melt marshmallows in milk. Cool; then add whipped cream. Put over crust and refrigerate. Dissolve strawberry jello in boiling water. Add strawberries. Let cool until thick. Pour over other layers. Chill. Cut in squares and enjoy!

Colored Mint Dessert

20 graham crackers, crushed
1/4 cup butter, melted
1 pint whipping cream, whipped

5 oz. colored pillow-mint candies
3 cups miniature colored marshmallows

Mix graham cracker crumbs and melted butter. Save 1/4 of mixture for top. Press remaining mixture into bottom of a 9x13" pan. Fold whipping cream, mints and marshmallows together and pour over graham cracker crust. Sprinkle remaining graham cracker crumb mixture over the top. Refrigerate overnight.

Marie Osmond's Killer Cheese Cake

1 package graham crackers
3 Tbsp. melted butter
2 Tbsp. + 3/4 cup sugar
24 oz. cream cheese, softened

3 eggs
1 tsp. + 1 Tbsp. vanilla
8 oz. sour cream
1 tsp. sugar

Crush the graham crackers. (I put them in a large zip-lock bag and let the kids crush them with a can. They love it!) Add 2 Tbsp. sugar and melted butter to crumbs. Press crust into cheese cake pan. Bake crust for 10 minutes at 350 degrees. Combine softened cream cheese and 3/4 cup sugar in a bowl; mix well. Add eggs, one at a time; then add 1 tsp. vanilla. Spoon filling over crust and bake for 1 hour at 300 degrees. Remove from oven and let sit for 10 minutes. Combine sour cream, 1 tsp. sugar and 1 Tbsp. vanilla. Spread over cheese cake and refrigerate at least 3 hours. Garnish with strawberries or fruit of your choice. Enjoy! (Note: I call this "Killer" Cheese Cake because it kills any diet you might have been on...but it's worth it!!)

Creamy Cheese Cake

16 oz. cream cheese, softened
2 cups evaporated milk, chilled
2 - 3 oz. pkg. lime jello
1 2/3 cups graham cracker crumbs

1 cup plus 1 Tbsp. sugar
1/4 cup margarine, melted
4 tsp. vanilla

Dissolve jello in 2 cups hot water. Let stand until cool. Mix graham cracker crumbs, 1 Tbsp. sugar and melted margarine. Reserve a little for the top and press remainder into 9x13" pan. Cream together the cream cheese, 1 cup sugar and vanilla. Whip chilled evaporated milk in larger bowl. Mix all ingredients together and pour on crust. Sprinkle reserved crumbs on top. Chill.

Easy Cheese Cake

3 cups graham cracker crumbs
1 cup sugar
1/2 cup margarine, melted

16 oz. cream cheese
1 cup sugar
4 cups Cool Whip

Blend together the graham cracker crumbs, sugar and melted margarine. Press into the bottom of a 9x13-inch pan. Blend the cream cheese and sugar; fold in Cool Whip. Spoon onto graham cracker crust and spread evenly. Chill at least 3 hours. Top with your favorite topping or fresh fruit.

Chocolate Cheesecake

1 1/2 cup vanilla wafer crumbs
6 Tbsp. butter, melted
3 Tbsp. sugar
24 oz. cream cheese
2 cups sugar
1 tsp. vanilla

1/2 tsp. rum flavoring
3 eggs
3 squares unsweetened chocolate, melted
6 oz. chocolate chips
10 oz. sour cream

Mix wafer crumbs, butter, and 3 Tbsp. sugar together and pat in bottom of 9 x 13 pan. Beat the cream cheese and 1 1/2 cups sugar together on high until creamy. Add the vanilla and rum. Blend well. Add eggs one at a time and the melted chocolate. After well blended, add the chocolate chips. Pour over wafer crumb crust. Bake 40 minutes at 350 degrees or until top cracks. Let cool 10 minutes. Mix sour cream with 1/2 cup sugar, and pour over top of cake, covering completely. Bake 10 minutes at 350 degrees. Refrigerate for at least 30 minutes before serving. For added decoration, drizzle with chocolate glaze or Hershey's chocolate syrup and garnish with raspberries or strawberry.

Cherry-Berries Dessert

6 egg whites
1/2 tsp. cream of tartar
1/4 tsp. salt
2 3/4 cups sugar
6 oz. cream cheese, softened
1 tsp. vanilla

2 cups whipping cream, whipped
2 cups miniature marshmallows
1 can (1 lb. 5 oz.) cherry pie filling
1 tsp. lemon juice
2 cups sliced fresh fruit

Heat oven to 275 degrees. Grease 9x13-inch pan. Beat egg whites, cream of tartar and salt until frothy. Gradually beat in 1 3/4 cups sugar. Beat until stiff and glassy, about 15 minutes. Spread in prepared pan. Bake 60 minutes. Turn oven off and leave meringue in oven until cool, about 12 hours or overnight. Mix cream cheese with 1 cup sugar and vanilla. Gently fold in whipped cream and marshmallows. Spread over meringue and refrigerate 12 hours or overnight. Cut into serving pieces and top with a mixture of cherry pie filling and lemon juice stirred into sliced fresh fruit (or frozen strawberries.)

Light as a Cloud Peach Dessert

1 angel food cake
3 1/2 oz. pkg. instant vanilla pudding
1 1/2 cups milk

6 oz. peach yogurt
1/3 cup sliced almonds, toasted
21 oz. can peach pie filling

Trim crust from angel food cake and tear into bite-sized pieces. Beat instant pudding mix with milk and stir in yogurt. In a 9x13" pan, layer half of the angel food pieces, then half of peach pie filling, and half of pudding mixture. Repeat layers. Garnish with sliced almond. Refrigerate 4 hours. Serves 12. This is recommended for low cholesterol diets.

Mom's Dessert

1/2 cup butter or margarine
1 cup flour
2 Tbsp. sugar
1/2 cup chopped pecans or walnuts
8 oz. cream cheese

1 cup powdered sugar
1 cup Cool Whip
2 pkg. instant pudding (any flavor)
3 cups milk

Grease 9x13" pan. Mix butter, flour and sugar. Add chopped nuts. Pat with hands into greased pan to form bottom layer. Bake 10-15 minutes at 325 degrees. Cool. Mix cream cheese, powdered sugar and Cool Whip. Pour over baked layer. Chill. Then mix instant pudding and milk. Pour over second layer. Top with Cool Whip.

Merry Mocha Dessert

2 cups crushed creme-filled chocolate
    sandwich cookies
1/4 cup margarine or butter, softened
16 oz. cream cheese, softened
7 oz. jar marshmallow creme

3 Tbsp. creme de cacao liqueur
3 Tbsp. coffee-flavored liqueur
2 cups whipping cream, whipped
1/4 cup chocolate-flavored syrup
1/4 cup chopped pecans

Lightly grease 9x13 pan. In small bowl, combine crushed sandwich cookies and margarine; mix well. Press mixture evenly in bottom of pan; refrigerate. In large bowl, beat cream cheese until light and fluffy. Add marshmallow creme; continue beating until smooth. Add liqueurs; mix gently to blend. Fold whipped cream into marshmallow mixture. Spoon filling evenly over crust. Drizzle chocolate syrup over filling; swirl with spoon. Sprinkle with pecans. Refrigerate until firm, about 4 hours. 20 servings.

Eclair Dessert

2 small pkg. vanilla instant pudding mix
3 cups milk
12 oz. Cool Whip
graham cracker squares
2 oz. squares chocolate

3 Tbsp. margarine
1/2 cup light corn syrup
1 tsp. vanilla
1 1/2 cups powdered sugar

Note:This should be made at least 12 hours before serving. Combine pudding mix and milk; mix until well blended, about 1-2 minutes. Add Cool Whip to pudding. In a 9x13-inch pan, place a layer of graham cracker squares to cover bottom. Put half of the pudding mixture over graham crackers. Then add another layer of graham cracker squares. Place remaining pudding mixture over graham crackers and add a third layer of graham cracker squares. Melt margarine and chocolate in saucepan. Add syrup, vanilla and powdered sugar. Stir together and spread over the top of the dessert. Refrigerate.

Lemon Bisque

3 oz. pkg. lemon jello
1 large can evaporated milk, well chilled
1 1/4 cups hot water
1/3 cup honey

1/8 tsp. salt
3 Tbsp. lemon juice
lemon rind
2 cups crushed vanilla wafers

Dissolve jello in hot water. Put in refrigerator until set. Whip evaporated milk. Add honey, salt, lemon juice and a little lemon rind. Whip jello and blend honey mixture with jello. Put half the crushed vanilla wafers in bottom of 9x13 pan, pour jello mixture over it, and sprinkle remaining crushed wafers on top. Refrigerate.

Angel Lemon Dessert

1 angel food cake
6 eggs, separated
1 1/2 cups sugar
3/4 cup lemon juice

1 Tbsp. grated lemon rind
1 env. plain gelatin
1/4 cup cold water

Beat egg yolks until light. Add 3/4 cup sugar, lemon juice and rind; cook in double boiler until thick. Mix envelope of plain gelatin in cold water. Add to cooked mixture while hot. Cool. Beat egg whites until stiff; fold in 3/4 cup sugar. Fold in lemon mixture. Break angel food cake into cubes and put in 9x13-inch pan. Pour lemon meringue mixture over the angel food cake pieces.

Cherry Dessert

2 cups graham cracker crumbs
1/4 cup margarine, melted
1 can sweetened condensed milk
1/4 cup lemon juice

1/2 tsp. almond flavoring
1 cup whipping cream, whipped
1 can cherry pie filling

Combine graham cracker crumbs and melted margarine. Press into the bottom of a 9x13-inch cake pan. Combine milk, lemon juice, and almond flavoring; mix well and spread on top of graham cracker crust. Spread whipping cream over all and top with the cherry pie filling. Refrigerate overnight.

Dirt Cake

1/4 cup butter or margarine
8 oz. cream cheese
1 cup powdered sugar
6 oz. pkg. instant vanilla pudding mix

2 1/2 cups milk
12 oz. Cool Whip
20 oz. Oreo cookies

Combine butter and cream cheese; cream well. Mix in powdered sugar and set aside. Mix together pudding mix and milk; set aside for 5 minutes. Add Cool Whip to cream cheese mixture; fold in pudding. Crush Oreos in blender. Alternately layer Oreo crumbs and pudding mixture in "flower pot" or "planter" (use white foam coffee cups), ending with Oreo crumbs on top. Refrigerate. Add silk flowers or plant and "gummy worms" as garnish when ready to serve. Makes 10-12 desserts.

Luxurious Frozen Mint Pie

2 cups (24) crushed cream-filled
    chocolate cookies
1/4 cup margarine, melted
1/4 cup milk

7 oz. marshmallow creme
few drops peppermint extract
few drops green food coloring
2 cups whipping cream, whipped

Combine crumbs and margarine; reserve 1/2 cup for topping. Press remaining crumb mixture onto bottom of 9-inch springform pan or pie plate. Chill. Gradually add milk to marshmallow creme, mixing until well blended. Add extract and food coloring; fold in whipped cream. Pour into pan; freeze until firm. Sprinkle with remaining crumbs or garnish with mint, if desired.

Poppy Seed Torte

1 cup crushed graham crackers
1 cup flour
1/2 chopped nuts
1/2 cup melted margarine or butter
5 egg yolks
1 1/2 cups milk
11/2 cup sugar

1/2 tsp. + 1/8 tsp. salt
1/4 cup poppy seed
2 Tbsp. corn starch
1 envelope plain gelatin
5 egg whites
1/2 tsp. cream of tartar
Cool Whip

Combine graham cracker crumbs, flour, chopped nuts and melted butter; mix well and pat in bottom of 9x13-inch pan. Bake 15 minutes at 325 degrees. Cool crust. Mix thoroughly egg yolks, milk, 1 cup sugar, 1/2 tsp. salt, poppy seed and corn starch and cook over medium heat, stirring constantly until thick. Remove from heat. Dissolve 1 envelope plain gelatin in 1/4 cup cold water and add to hot filling. Stir until thoroughly mixed. Cool filling. (For faster cooling, set pan in a larger pan of cold water; stir often.) Beat 5 egg whites with 1/8 tsp. salt and cream of tartar until foamy. Gradually add 1/2 cup sugar and beat at high speed until thick and glossy. Stir into cold filling and pour on crust. Cover with a thin layer of Cool Whip; sprinkle with chopped nuts, if desired. Cover with foil and freeze. Cut in 24 squares to serve. Let dessert thaw slightly before serving, about 10-15 minutes.

Frosty Strawberry Dessert

1 cup flour
1/4 cup brown sugar
1/2 cup chopped walnuts
1/2 cup melted butter
2 egg whites

2 cups sliced strawberries (fresh or frozen)
1 cup white sugar
2 Tbsp. lemon juice
1 cup whipping cream

Mix flour, brown sugar, chopped nuts and melted butter. Put 2/3 of mixture in bottom of 9x13 pan. Bake at 350 degrees for 20 minutes. Beat together at high speed for 10 minutes: egg whites, strawberries, white sugar and lemon juice. Whip 1 cup whipping cream. Fold into strawberry mixture. Pour over crumbs. Top with remaining crumbs. Garnish with sliced strawberries. Cover and freeze overnight. May be made 2 days ahead of serving time.

Pumpkin Pie

2 eggs, slightly beaten
1 can (16 oz.) pumpkin
3/4 cup sugar
1/2 tsp salt

1 tsp. cinnamon
1/2 tsp. ginger
1/4 tsp. cloves
13 oz. evaporated milk or light cream

Mix ingredients and pour into 9-inch deep pie shell or 2 frozen pie shells. Bake at 425 degrees for 15 minutes. Reduce temperature to 350 degrees and bake another 45 minutes or until knife inserted in center comes out clean.

Perfect Pumpkin Pie

1 cup pumpkin
1 cup brown sugar
1 tsp. cinnamon
1 tsp. allspice
1/2 tsp. cloves

1/4 tsp. ginger
1 cup sweet milk
3 eggs
1 crust pie shell(s)

Mix pumpkin, sugar and spices thoroughly before adding milk. Separate eggs and add beaten egg yolks. Gently fold in the stiffly beaten egg whites. Makes 1 large or 2 small pies. Salt, if desired. Bake at 450 degrees for 10 minutes; reduce to 325 degrees for 30 minutes.

Zucchini Pie

4 cups zucchini
1 1/4 cups sugar or 1 cup honey
2 Tbsp. flour
1 1/2 tsp. cinnamon
1 1/2 tsp. cream of tartar

2 Tbsp. lemon juice
dash of salt
dash of nutmeg
butter to dot pie
double crust pie shell

Peel, seed and slice zucchini. Boil in water until tender. Drain. Let stand in cold water 5 minutes. Drain. Add all remaining ingredients, except butter. Mix well. Place in double crust pie. Dot with butter. Bake at 400 degrees for 40 to 50 minutes. This tastes like apple pie!

Rhubarb Pie

Pastry for 2-crust pie
2 cups rhubarb
1 cup sugar

2 Tbsp. flour
2 eggs
1 Tbsp. orange juice

Cut rhubarb into 1/2 inch pieces. Beat eggs very slightly. Add sugar and flour to the eggs. Combine with rhubarb. Add orange juice. Line pie pan with pastry dough. Put rhubarb mixture into the unbaked pastry shell. Cover with strips of pastry dough, put on in criss-cross fashion. Bake at 450 degrees for 10 minutes. Reduce heat to 350 degrees and continue baking for 30 minutes.

Sunrise Cherry Pie

8.25 oz. can crushed pineapple
8 oz. cream cheese, softened
1/2 tsp. vanilla
21 oz. can cherry pie filling

1 cup whipping cream
1/4 cup powdered sugar
1 graham cracker pie crust

Drain pineapple well, reserving 2 Tbsp. syrup. Combine softened cream cheese, vanilla and reserved syrup, mixing until well blended. Stir in 1/4 cup pineapple and 1/2 cup pie filling. Gradually add sugar to cream, beating until soft peaks form. Fold into cream cheese mixture. Pour into crust. Top with remaining pineapple around the outside edge of top and remaining cherry pie filling in center of top. Chill until firm.

Raspberry Pie

1 crust pie shell
24 marshmallows
1 cup milk

1 cup whipping cream, whipped
2 cups raspberries

Heat marshmallows and milk together until marshmallows are melted; cool. Add whipped cream and raspberries. Spoon into pie shell. Refrigerate.

Light 'N' Fruity Pie

3 oz. pkg. strawberry jello (or other flavor)
2/3 cup boiling water
2 cups ice cubes
8 oz. Cool Whip
1 graham cracker pie crust

1 cup fresh fruit (sliced strawberries,
   peaches, bananas, raspberries or
   blueberries) or 1 can apricots, peaches,
   fruit cocktail or crushed pineapple,
   drained

Dissolve gelatin completely in boiling water, stirring about 3 minutes. Add ice cubes and stir until gelatin is thickened, about 2 to 3 minutes. Remove any unmelted ice. Blend in Cool Whip; whip until smooth. Fold in fruit. Chill, if necessary, until mixture will mound. Spoon into crust. Chill 2 hours. Garnish, if desired, with fresh fruit.

Key Lime Pie

1/3 cup sugar
1 envelope unflavored gelatin
1/4 cup fresh lime juice
3 egg yolks, slightly beaten
2 tsp. grated lime peel

2 cups whipping cream
1/8 tsp. green food coloring
1 9-inch graham cracker pie shell or
   baked pie shell

In top of double boiler, mix sugar and gelatin. Combine lime juice and egg yolks and blend into sugar mixture. Cook over simmering water until thick, stirring constantly. Remove from heat, stir in lime peel and cool. Whip cream with food coloring until stiff and fold into gelatin lime mixture. Pour into crust. Chill until firm.

Pecan Pie

2 Tbsp. butter
1/2 cup light brown sugar
2 eggs
2 Tbsp. flour
1/4 tsp. salt

1/2 tsp. vanilla
1 cup light corn syrup
1 1/2 cups broken pecan pieces
1 crust pie shell

Preheat oven to 350 degrees. Cream butter and sugar until light. Add eggs, one at a time, beating well after each; then add flour, salt, vanilla, and syrup, blending thoroughly until smooth. Mix in pecans. Pour into pie shell and bake at 350 degrees about 35 minutes. The middle will still wriggle, but will solidify as it cools.

Soda Cracker Pie

14 soda crackers, crushed
3 egg whites
1/2 tsp. baking powder
1 cup sugar
1/2 cup chopped walnuts

1 1/2 tsp. vanilla
1 cup whipping cream
1/2 cup sugar
1 tsp. vanilla
10 oz. fresh or frozen strawberries, drained

Beat egg whites until stiff; fold in 1 cup sugar, 1 1/2 tsp. vanilla, crackers, baking powder and walnuts. Pour into 9-inch pie pan. Bake for 30 minutes at 350 degrees. When cooled, whip cream; fold in 1/2 cup sugar and 1 tsp. vanilla. Put whipped cream and strawberries on crust and refrigerate 4 hours.

Swedish Nut Cracker Pie

4 eggs, separated
1 cup sugar
12 soda crackers, crushed
1 cup chopped nuts

1 tsp. vanilla
fruit
whipped or ice cream

Beat egg whites until stiff and set aside. Beat egg yolks until fluffy, gradually beating in sugar. Add crackers, nuts and vanilla. Fold in egg whites. Spread in a 9x9-inch pan or pie plate. Bake at 350 degrees about 30 minutes. Serve with fruit and whipped cream or ice cream.

Lemon Forsythia Pie

1 cup flour
1/2 cup soft butter or margarine
2 Tbsp. sugar
1/4 tsp. salt
2 egg whites

2/3 cup sugar
2 tsp. grated lemon peel
1/4 cup fresh lemon juice
drop of yellow food coloring
1/2 pint whipping cream, whipped stiff

Combine flour, 1/2 cup margarine, 2 Tbsp. sugar and salt; mix together with fork or hands until crumbly. Save about 1/3 of mixture for use later. Press remainder into greased and floured pie plate. Bake at 375 degrees for 12-15 minutes. Also spread the remaining 1/3 crumb mixture on a cookie sheet and bake at the same time. This might brown faster than the mixture in pie plate so be sure to watch this. Cool. Beat egg whites until stiff; add 2/3 cup sugar, lemon peel, lemon juice and food coloring and continue beating until stiff. Fold in whipped cream. Put into shell and top with crumbs. Chill or freeze, either works fine. Can be served with strawberries or raspberries on top.

Swedish Angel Lemon Pie

4 egg whites
1/4 tsp. cream of tartar
1 cup sugar
4 egg yolks

1/4 cup sugar
juice and grated rind of 1 lemon
1 cup whipping cream, whipped

Beat the egg whites until frothy, then add cream of tartar. Beat until stiff and then gradually add 1 cup sugar. Spread in a buttered 9-inch pie pan and bake at 300 degrees for about 25 minutes or until merangue is set and slightly brown. Beat egg yolks until thick. Add 1/4 cup sugar, lemon juice and rind. Cook in double boiler, stirring until thickened. (If after cooling the filling becomes too think, add 2 Tbsp. of hot water.) When merangue and filling are cool, whip the cream. Blend 1/2 of the whipped cream with the filling and spread over merangue. Spread with remaining whipped cream. Serves 8.

Brownie Pie

2 eggs
1 cup sugar
1/2 cup butter, softened
1/2 cup flour

3 Tbsp. cocoa
1 tsp. vanilla
pinch of salt
1/2 cup chopped walnuts or pecans

In mixer bowl, combine eggs, sugar, butter, flour, cocoa, vanilla and salt. Beat with electric mixer for 4 minutes. Stir in chopped nuts. Spoon into buttered pie pan. Bake 30 minutes at 325 degrees. Pie settles like meringue as it cools. Serve with whipped cream or ice cream.

German Sweet Chocolate Cream Pie

4 oz. German sweet chocolate
1/3 cup milk
2 Tbsp. sugar

3 oz. cream cheese, softened
8 oz. Cool Whip
1 graham cracker pie crust

Heat chocolate and 2 Tbsp. milk over low heat, stirring until melted. Beat sugar into cream cheese; add remaining milk and chocolate mixture, beat until smooth. Fold Cool Whip into chocolate mixture and blend until smooth. Spoon mixture into crust. Freeze about 4 hours. Garnish with chocolate curls, if desired.

Glorified Butterscotch Pie

1/3 cup peanut butter
1 cup graham cracker crumbs
1 cup brown sugar
4 Tbsp. butter
1/3 cup flour
1/2 tsp. salt

2 eggs yolks
2 cups milk, scalded
1/4 tsp. vanilla
4 Tbsp. sugar
1 cup whipping cream, whipped

Blend peanut butter and graham cracker crumbs. Line pie plate, including sides, with mixture and chill. Mix sugar, flour and salt. Gradually stir in scalded milk. Cook in double boiler over boiling water 10 minutes, stirring constantly until thick. Stir small amount into egg yolks and then add to cooked filling. Cook 2 minutes longer. Add butter, vanilla and cool. Pour into pie shell and cover with whipped cream.

Cream Puffs

1/2 cup water
1/4 cup butter or margarine
1/8 tsp. salt
1/2 cup flour

2 large eggs
Custard Filling, (follows this recipe)
Chocolate Glaze, (follows this recipe)
confectioners' sugar

Preheat oven to 400 degrees. In small saucepan, combine water, butter and salt. Over medium heat, bring to boiling. Remove from heat. Immediately, with wooden spoon, beat in all the flour. Over low heat, beat until mixture leaves side of pan and forms a ball, about 1 to 2 minutes. Remove from heat. Add l egg; with portable electric mixer or wooden spoon, beat until well blended. Then add other egg, and beat until the dough is shiny and satiny, about 1 minute. Drop the dough by rounded tablespoonfuls, 2 inches apart, onto an ungreased cookie sheet. Bake 35 to 40 minutes, or until puffed and golden-brown. Puffs should sound hollow when lightly tapped with fingertip. Meanwhile, make Custard Filling. Carefully remove puffs to wire rack. Let cool completely, away from drafts. Shortly before serving: cut off top of cream puffs with sharp knife. With fork, gently remove any soft dough from the insde. Fill puffs with custard; replace tops. Frost tops with Chocolate Glaze, or spinkle with confectioners' sugar. Serve soon after filling, as filled puffs become soggy on standing. Makes 6 large puffs. (For miniature puffs, drop batter by teaspoonfuls, 2 inches apart, and bake 20 to 25 minutes at 400 degrees. Fill and frost as above for dessert, or fill with savory filling for hors d'oeuvres.)

Custard Filling for Cream Puffs

1 pkg. (3 oz) vanilla pudding mix
1 1/2 cups milk
1/2 cup heavy cream

2 Tbsp. confectioners' sugar
1/2 tsp. vanilla extract

Make pudding as package label directs, using 1 1/2 cups milk. Pour into medium bowl; place waxed paper directly on surface. Refrigerate until chilled, at least one hour. In small bowl, combine heavy cream, sugar, and vanilla; with rotary beater, beat just until stiff. Then fold whipped-cream mixture into pudding until combined. Refrigerate several hours, to chill well before using. Makes 2 cups; enough to fill 6 large or 36 miniature puffs.

Chocolate Glaze for Cream Puffs

1/2 cup semisweet chocolate pieces
1 Tbsp. shortening

1 Tbsp. light corn syrup
1 1/2 Tbsp. milk

In top of double boiler, combine all ingredients. Place over hot, not boiling, water, stirring occasionally, until mixture is smooth and well blended. Let cool slightly before using to frost puffs. Makes 1/2 cup.

Choc-O-Mint Crepe Filling

1/2 gallon vanilla ice cream
1/2 pint whipping cream
1 Tbsp. powdered sugar

1 tsp. vanilla
cream de menthe
shaved chocolate

Beat whipping cream, gradually adding powdered sugar and vanilla. Cut ice cream into logs about 5" long and 1" in diameter. Lightly sprinkle crepe with shaved chocolate. Place ice cream log on crepe. Wrap crepe. Top with sweetened whipped cream and drizzle creme de menthe across top. Garnish with additional shaved chocolate or maraschino cherry.

Strawberry Cream Crepe Filling

4 cups fresh strawberries, sliced
2 Tbsp. sugar
14 oz. can sweetened condensed milk
1/4 cup lemon juice

1/2 cup whipping cream, whipped
12 dessert crepes
whipped cream for garnish
12 whole strawberries for garnish

Sprinkle sliced strawberries with sugar and set aside. Beat condensed milk with lemon juice until thick. Fold in strawberries and whipped cream. Divide between crepes and fold. Garnish with additional whipped cream and a strawberry centered on cream. Note: 20 oz. frozen strawberries could be substituted for the fresh berries. Drain off juice and omit the 2 Tbsp. sugar.

Custard

1/2 cup sugar
1/4 cup boiling water
4 eggs

1 cup sweetened condensed milk
1 cup warm water or milk

Melt sugar in saucepan over low heat; remove from heat. Add boiling water; stir until dissolved. Pour in metal ring mold or pan. Coat bottom and sides of pan as much as possible with this sugar mixture. Beat eggs; add sweetened condensed milk and warm water or milk. Pour into sugar coated pan. Put this pan into a bigger pan of water and bake at 350 degrees for 1 hour. It is done when a knife inserted 1-inch from edge comes out clean. To serve, invert.

Dad's Great Grape Tapioca Pudding

3/4 cup Minute Tapioca
2 cups water
48 oz. bottle grape juice

1 cup sugar
2 Tbsp. vanilla

Put 2 cups water and 2 cups grape juice into a 4-quart saucepan; add tapioca and heat on medium heat, stirring constantly. When mixture starts to bubble, add the remaining grape juice, stirring constantly. Add sugar and vanilla; cook until it is thoroughly heated. Remove from heat and let it cool. The pudding will thicken as it cools. Serve plain or with Cool Whip on top.

Mom's Swedish Rice Pudding

1 heaping cup medium grain rice
1/2 gallon whole milk
6 egg yolks (as you separate eggs, leave a
   little of the whites, too)

1 cup sugar
1/2 tsp. salt
1 Tbsp. vanilla
2 tsp. lemon flavoring

Rinse 1 heaping cup of medium grain rice (not instant rice). Heat milk; add rice. Cook rice and milk until rice is soft. Beat 6 egg yolks. Add sugar and salt to rice when soft. Add beaten egg yolks and stir fast to whip pudding. Add vanilla and lemon flavoring. Remove from heat. As pudding cools, fluff every 10 minutes or so. Great warm or cold.

Baked Peach Pudding

2 cups sliced raw peaches
3/4 cup + 1 cup sugar
1/2 cup milk
4 Tbsp. margarine
1/2 tsp. baking powder

1 cup flour
1 Tbsp. cornstarch
1/4 tsp. salt
1 cup boiling water

Place sliced peaches in a greased 9x13-inch pan. Combine 3/4 cup sugar and margarine. Add baking powder, flour and milk. Spread over peaches. Mix 1 cup sugar, cornstarch and salt. Sprinkle this mixture over batter in pan. Pour boiling water over all and bake at 325 degrees for 50 minutes. Serve warm with cream. (This is a cross between cobbler and pudding. You can also use rhubarb and apples.)

Hot Fudge Pudding

1 cup cake flour
2 tsp. baking powder
1/4 tsp. salt
3/4 cup sugar
2 Tbsp. cocoa
1/2 cup milk

2 Tbsp. butter or margarine, melted
1 cup chopped nuts
1 cup brown sugar, packed
1/4 cup cocoa
1 3/4 cups hot water

Heat oven to 350 degrees. Sift flour, baking powder, salt, sugar and 2 Tbsp. cocoa into bowl. Stir in milk and melted butter. Blend in nuts. Spread in 9x9-inch square pan. Combine brown sugar and 1/4 cup cocoa and sprinkle over the top. Pour hot water over entire batter. Bake 45 minutes. During baking, cake mixture rises to top and chocolate sauce settles to bottom. Serve warm, spooned into saucedishes, with whipped cream. 9 servings.

CORY

Eric was just turning three when Mark and I decided it was time for a little brother or sister. Other than being tired, I have pretty easy pregnancies. I guess I was made for having babies. About six weeks before my due date, I went in for a check-up and told the doctor I had been feeling rather crampy for three days. He checked me out and, sure enough, the baby was coming. That was my last night of work, and I went on two weeks bedrest and medicine to stop the contractions. It worked, because two days after I finished the medicine, I had little Corbin (Cory) Roe! Less than four hours of labor and he was born four weeks early, weighing 7 lbs. 11 oz. It's a good thing my babies come early or they would be nine pounders easily! He, too, was very healthy and looked exactly like Eric did at birth. It was like seeing Eric born all over again.

Born June 9, 1991, I was able to take him on walks outside in the summertime and it made my maternity leave more enjoyable than when Eric was born in Minnesota, going into the winter.

Cory is all boy. He's built a little stockier than Eric and is much more interested in bats and balls and any kind of sports than Eric has ever been. He seems a bit more outgoing than Eric and yet he has a very easy-going personality, too. Neither of the boys are what I'd call "rowdy boys," but rather a bit timid and cautious. Mark and I were both like that when we were growing up, so we understand it well. Both boys love to sing and read books. Mark and I sing to them each night before bedtime. We all pray together and then kiss each other goodnight. I thank God each and every day for the two special blessings He has entrusted in our care. I love coming home from work and hearing the boys call out, "Mommy, Mommy, you're home! I love you, Mommy."

"I love you, too, Eric! I love you, too, Cory! You are Mommy's special blessings!"

Cory

Cory
and Eric
are best buddies.

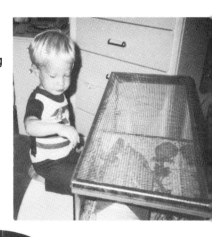

Cory checking out one of his "pets."

I love spending time with my "special blessings."

Cakes & Frostings

Black Forest Cherry Bundt Cake

1 pkg. chocolate cake mix
1 - 21 oz. can cherry pie filling

1/4 cup oil
3 eggs

Combine cake mix, pie filling, oil and eggs. Beat well until smooth. Pour into a greased and floured 12-cup Bundt pan. Bake in preheated 350 degree oven for 45 minutes or until done. Cool in pan 25 minutes, then invert onto rack to finish cooling. Decorate and serve with 1 can cherry pie filling and whipped cream. Note: This is really pretty to serve at a party. Cut the cake first, then top with cherry pie filling, then whipped cream. It looks great and is easy for guests to serve themselves at a buffet.

Maraschino Cherry Cake

1/2 cup shortening
1 1/2 cup sugar
2 cups plus 6 Tbsp. cake flour
1/2 cup chopped nuts
16 maraschino cherries, cut in quarters

3 tsp. baking powder
1/4 tsp. salt
3/4 cup liquid (1/4 cup liquid from jar of
    cherries plus 1/2 cup milk)
4 egg whites, stiffly beaten

Cream sugar and shortening thoroughly. Mix nuts and cherries and dredge with 2 Tbsp. flour. Mix remainder of flour with baking powder and salt. Add to creamed mixture alternately with the liquid. Blend in floured nuts and cherries. Fold in egg whites, stiffly beaten. Bake 50 minutes at 350 degrees in a 9x13 pan or 30 minutes in two 8-inch layers. Nice to serve at February parties.

Dump Cake

1 medium can crushed pineapple,
    with juice
1/2 cup sugar
1 can cherry pie filling

1 box yellow cake mix
1/2 cup butter or margarine
1/2 cup nuts, chopped

Grease 9x13-inch pan. Spread pineapple, including juice, over the bottom of the pan. Cover evenly with sugar. Add cherry pie filling. Spread evenly over pineapple and sugar. Sprinkle cake mix evenly over mixture. Slice butter and place evenly over top of cake mix. Sprinkle chopped nuts over the top. Bake at 350 degrees for 1 hour.

Cherry Chocolate Cake

1 pkg. chocolate cake mix
3 eggs
21 oz. can cherry pie filling
1 tsp. almond extract

5 Tbsp. butter
1 cup sugar
1/3 cup milk
6 oz. chocolate chips

Combine cake mix, eggs, cherry pie filling and almond extract. Bake in greased and floured 9x13-inch pan for 35-40 minutes, or large sheet pan for 20 minutes. Combine butter, sugar and milk; boil for 1 minute. Add chocolate chips. Frost cake; top with crushed walnuts. For a "Rocky Road" frosting, top warm cake with miniature marshmallows before topping with chocolate frosting and chopped walnuts.

Chocolate Cherry Cheese Torte

1 pkg. Swiss Chocolate cake mix
1 can cherry pie filling
4 oz. cream cheese

2 tsp. lemon juice
1 can creamy vanilla frosting

Prepare cake as directed on package. Bake in two 8-inch round pans. Cool. Split each cake layer into two thin layers. For cream cheese frosting, beat cream cheese and lemon juice until smooth. Fold in vanilla frosting. Spread a thin layer of frosting and pie filling between all layers and on top of cake. Store cake in refrigerator until ready to serve.

Apple Cake

1 1/3 cup sugar
3/4 cup shortening
2 eggs
3/4 cup warm water
2 1/4 cup flour
1/2 tsp. salt

1 tsp. soda
1 tsp. cinnamon
1/2 cup chopped nuts
3 cups apple slices
3/4 cup brown sugar

Cream sugar, shortening and eggs. Add warm water, then flour, salt, soda and cinnamon. Mix well. Fold in nuts and apple slices. Pour into 9x13 cake pan. Top with brown sugar. Bake 30-35 minutes at 350 degrees. Frost with Butterscotch Sauce.

Apple Chip Cake

1 1/2 cups vegetable oil
2 cups sugar
2 eggs
3 cups chopped apples (about 3 apples)
1 tsp. soda

3 cups flour
2 tsp. vanilla
1/2 tsp. salt
1 tsp. cinnamon
1/2 cup chopped nuts

Combine oil, sugar and eggs. Add dry ingredients and continue to mix. Add remaining ingredients, stirring by hand, as batter is very stiff. Bake in 9x13 pan at 350 degrees for 45 minutes. Serve plain or with ice cream.

Applesauce Cake

1/2 cup soft shortening
2 cups sugar
1 extra-large egg
1 1/2 cups applesauce
2 1/2 cups flour
1 1/2 tsp. soda

1 1/2 tsp. salt
3/4 tsp. each cinnamon, cloves, allspice
1/2 cup water
1/2 cup chopped walnuts
1 cup raisins

Cream shortening and sugar. Beat in egg and applesauce until thoroughly blended. Add water, then flour, soda, salt and spices. Blend; then add walnuts and raisins. Pour into 9x13 pan and bake at 350 degrees for 45 minutes.

Fruit Cocktail Cake

1 1/2 cups flour
1 cup sugar
1 tsp. salt
1 tsp. soda
1 egg, beaten

1 No. 2 can fruit cocktail, with juice
1 tsp. vanilla
1 cup brown sugar
1/2 cup chopped pecans or walnuts

Blend flour, sugar, salt and soda. Add beaten egg, fruit cocktail (with juice) and vanilla. Mix and pour into greased and floured 9x13" pan. Sprinkle with brown sugar and chopped nuts. Bake 40 minutes at 350 degrees.

Wilderness Pie Cake

1 can pie filling, any flavor
2 cups flour
1 3/4 cup sugar
2/3 cup vegetable oil
2 eggs, beaten

1 tsp. vanilla
2 tsp. cinnamon
1 1/2 tsp. baking soda
3/4 cup nuts, chopped
1 1/2 Tbsp. butter, melted

Combine 1 cup sugar, oil, eggs, vanilla; beat well. Add pie filling, flour, 1 tsp. cinnamon, soda and nuts. Mix well. Pour into 9x13" cake pan. Top with mixture of 3/4 cup sugar, 1 tsp. cinnamon, and melted butter. Bake at 350 degrees for 40 minutes.

Banana Cake

2 1/2 cups flour
1 2/3 cups sugar
1 1/4 tsp. baking powder
1 1/4 tsp. soda
1 tsp. salt

2/3 cup soft shortening
2/3 cup sour milk
1 1/4 cup mashed bananas (3-4)
2 large eggs

Blend together flour, sugar, baking powder, soda and salt. Add shortening, sour milk and mashed bananas and beat two minutes. Add eggs and beat 2 minutes more. Bake at 350 degrees for 35-40 minutes. (P.S. To make sour milk, add a little lemon juice to milk.)

Banana-Date Cake

3 overripe large bananas
2 1/2 cup flour
1 cup sugar
1 tsp. baking powder
1 tsp. baking soda
1/2 tsp. salt

3/4 cup butter or margarine, softened
1/2 cup sour cream
3 eggs
1 cup chopped dates
1 cup chopped walnuts
powdered sugar

Heat oven to 350 degrees. Grease and flour 9x13-inch pan. Puree bananas in blender or food processor, making 1 1/2 cups. Combine all ingredients except dates, nuts and powdered sugar in large bowl of mixer. Beat on low speed, scraping bowl occasionally, for 3 minutes. Pour into pan. Stir in dates and walnuts. Bake until wooden pick inserted in center comes out clean, 40 to 50 minutes; cool. Sprinkle lightly with powdered sugar. Makes 12 to 15 servings.

Orange Cake

1/2 cup butter	2 cups flour
1 cup sugar	1 tsp. vanilla
1 egg	1 tsp. baking soda
rind of 1 orange, grated	1/2 tsp. salt
1/2 cup chopped raisins	juice of 1 orange
1 cup sour milk	1 1/2 cups sugar

Cream together the butter and 1 cup sugar; add egg, orange rind, sour milk and vanilla. Blend well. Add flour, soda and salt; fold in raisins. Pour into 9x13-inch pan. Bake at 350 degrees for 45 to 50 minutes. When done, cool for 5 minutes. Combine orange juice and 1 1/2 cups sugar; mix well and pour over cake.

Zucchini Chocolate Cake

1/2 cup margarine, softened	4 Tbsp. sifted cocoa
1/2 cup vegetable oil	1/2 tsp. baking powder
1 3/4 cups sugar	1 tsp. baking soda
2 eggs	1/2 tsp. cinnamon
1 tsp. vanilla	1/2 tsp. cloves
1/2 cup sour milk	2 cups finely diced, peeled zucchini
2 1/2 cups flour	12 oz. chocolate chips

Cream margarine, oil and sugar. Add eggs, vanilla and sour milk and beat until blended. Add remaining ingredients, except zucchini and chocolate chips, and beat until well blended. Stir in zucchini. Pour into greased and floured 9x13" pan. Sprinkle on chocolate chips. Bake at 325 degrees for 40-45 minutes.

Coconut Cake

1 pkg. yellow cake mix (2-layer size)	1/4 cup oil
1 small pkg. vanilla instant pudding mix	2 cups flake coconut
1 1/3 cups water	1 cup chopped walnuts or pecans
4 eggs	

Blend cake mix, pudding mix, water, eggs and oil in large mixer bowl. Beat at medium speed 4 minutes. Stir in coconut and chopped nuts. Pour into 3 greased and floured 9-inch layer pans. Bake at 350 degrees for 35 minutes. Cool in pans 15 minutes; remove and cool on rack. Fill and frost with Coconut Cream Cheese Frosting.

Carrot Cake

2 cups sugar
2 cups flour
2 tsp. soda
2 tsp. baking powder
2 tsp. cinnamon
1 1/4 cups oil
4 eggs

2 cups raw grated carrots
8 oz. cream cheese, softened
1/2 cup margarine, softened
1 lb. powdered sugar
2 tsp. vanilla
1/2 cup chopped nuts

Mix together white sugar, flour, soda, baking powder and cinnamon. Add oil and carrots; mix well. Add eggs, one at a time, beating well after every addition. Pour into greased and floured 9x13 pan. Bake for 1 hour at 350 degrees. Beat together the cream cheese, margarine and vanilla; add powdered sugar and mix well. Spread on chilled cake. Sprinkle chopped nuts on top, if desired.

Chocolate Oatmeal Cake

1 cup oatmeal
1 1/2 cups boiling water
3/4 cup white sugar
3/4 cup brown sugar
1/3 cup vegetable oil
4 egg whites

1/2 cup cocoa
1 1/2 cups flour
1 tsp. baking soda
1/2 tsp. salt
1 tsp. vanilla

Preheat oven to 350 degrees. Pour boiling water over oatmeal. Set aside to cool (approx. 30 minutes.) Combine sugars and oil. Beat egg whites for approximately 10 seconds. Add to sugar/oil mixture. Combine flour, cocoa, baking soda and salt. Add dry mixture to oil mixture. Combine, but do not overbeat. Add vanilla and stir. Add oatmeal mixture to batter. Bake in 9x13 pan, sprayed with non-stock cooking spray, for 30-35 minutes, or until wooden pick inserted in center comes out clean. Frost with Dessert Icing or dust with powdered sugar. This is very tasty and is recommended for low-fat, low cholesterol diets.

Triple Chocolate Cake

1 pkg. chocolate cake mix
1 3/4 cups milk
1 pkg. instant chocolate pudding mix

2 eggs
12 oz. chocolate chips

Combine all ingredients; mix by hand until well blended, about 2 minutes. Pour into greased and floured bundt or tube pan. Bake at 350 degree oven for 50-55 minutes or until cake springs back when lightly pressed. Do not overbake. Cool 15 minutes in pan. Remove from pan and cool on rack.

Ho Ho Cake

2 - 8 or 9-inch chocolate cake layers
2 cups milk
5 Tbsp. flour
2 cups sugar

1 cup margarine
1 cup solid shortening
1 tsp. vanilla
6 oz. chocolate chips

Combine 1 1/2 cups milk and 5 Tbsp. flour in saucepan. Cook until paste. In mixer bowl, combine 1 cup sugar, 1/2 cup margarine, and shortening. Beat until creamy; add vanilla and mix well. Add cooled paste and beat 7 minutes. Spread between chocolate cake layers and refrigerate 1 hour. In saucepan, combine 1 cup sugar, 1/2 cup milk and 1/2 cup margarine. Bring to boiling; boil for 2 minutes. Add chocolate chips; stir until melted. Pour over top of cake and refrigerate.

Chocolate Thunder Cake

1 pkg. German Chocolate cake mix
14 oz. sweetened condensed milk
1 jar fudge ice cream topping

16 oz. Cool Whip
2 Heath candy bars

Bake cake in a 9x13-inch pan as directed on box. Let cool 25-30 minutes. Poke holes in cake with wooden spoon handle. Pour on sweetened condensed milk, spread evenly. Wait 5 minutes. Spread fudge topping over cake. Wait 5 minutes. Spread Cool Whip over cake and sprinkle crushed candy bars over the top.

Chocolate Surprise Cake

1 chocolate cake mix
3 oz. pkg. cherry jello
1 cup boiling water
1 cup 7-Up

1 box instant pudding mix, any flavor
1 cup milk
8 oz. Cool Whip

Prepare chocolate cake according to package directions. When cool, poke holes in top of cake with fork. Dissolve the cherry jello in boiling water and add 7-Up. Pour over cake. Whip together the instant pudding mix and milk. Fold in Cool Whip and frost cake. Store in refrigerator.

Mohogany Chiffon

3/4 cup boiling water
1/2 cup cocoa
1 3/4 cups flour
1 3/4 cups sugar
1 1/2 tsp. soda
1 tsp. salt

1/2 cup vegetable oil
7 unbeaten egg yolks
2 tsp. vanilla
1 cup egg whites (7 or 8)
1/2 tsp. cream of tartar

Heat oven to 325 degrees. Combine boiling water and cocoa, let cool. Blend flour, sugar, soda, and salt in bowl. Make a well and add oil, egg yolks, vanilla, and cocoa mixture. Beat until smooth. Measure egg whites and cream of tartar into large mixing bowl and beat until very stiff. Pour egg yolk mixture in thin stream over entire surface of egg whites, gently cutting and folding in with rubber spatula until completely blended. Pour into ungreased 10" tube pan. Bake 55 minutes at 325 degrees, then at 350 degrees for 10 to 15 minutes more. Invert; let hang until cool. Ice with Brown Beauty Icing.

EZ Cake

1 cup sugar
2 cups flour
2 tsp. baking soda
4 Tbsp. cocoa

1 cup cold water
1 cup salad dressing
2 tsp. vanilla

Grease and flour 9x13 pan. Combine all ingredients and mix well. Bake at 350 degrees for 30 minutes. Frost with EZ Frosting.

Turtle Cake

1 box German chocolate cake mix
3/4 cup margarine
1/2 cup condensed milk
14 oz. caramels

1 cup chopped pecans
2/3 cup chocolate chips
sour cream chocolate frosting

Mix cake mix as directed on box. Pour half of the batter in a greased and floured 9x13-inch pan. Bake 15 minutes at 350 degrees. While this is baking, melt caramels, milk and margarine (in T-Fal sauce pan, if possible); pour over baked half cake. Sprinkle pecans and chocolate chips over caramel sauce. Pour remaining batter over this and bake 20 minutes more. Ice with sour cream chocolate frosting or serve with ice cream.

Chocolate Chip Date Cake

8 oz. dates
1 1/2 cups boiling water
1 1/2 tsp. baking soda
2/3 cup shortening
1 1/2 cups sugar
2 eggs
1 tsp. vanilla

2 cups flour
3/4 tsp. salt
2 Tbsp. cocoa
4 Tbsp. brown sugar
1/2 cup chopped nuts
6 oz. chocolate chips

Cut up dates; add boiling water and soda. Cool. Cream shortening and white sugar; add eggs and vanilla. Sift flour, salt and cocoa; add this to creamed mixture. Fold in date mixture. Pour into 9x13-inch cake pan. Top with brown sugar, chopped nuts and chocolate chips. Bake at 350 degrees for 35 minutes.

Lemon Cake

1 pkg. lemon cake mix
1 pkg. instant lemon pudding
3/4 cup water
3/4 cup oil

4 eggs
1/2 cup lemon or orange juice
2 cups powdered sugar

Combine lemon cake mix, pudding mix, water and oil. Mix and beat 5 minutes. Add eggs, one at a time, and beat 5 minutes more. Bake 40 minutes at 325 degrees in a greased and floured 9x13 pan. When done, prick the top of the cake. Mix fruit juice and powdered sugar. Pour over cake while still warm.

Yellow Lemon Cake

1 pkg. yellow cake mix
1 pkg (3.75 oz.) instant lemon pudding
4 eggs

1/4 cup salad oil
1 cup water

Combine and blend all ingredients. Beat at medium speed for 2 minutes. Pour into greased and floured 9x13" pan. Bake at 350 degrees for 45-50 minutes. Cool in pan 15 minutes; then cool on rack. Sprinkle with confectioners' sugar. For sugar design, place paper doilies on the cake before sprinkling with powdered sugar; then carefully lift off doilies.

Lemon Coconut Cake

4 eggs
2 cups sugar
2 cups flour
2 tsp. baking powder

1 tsp. vanilla
1 cup hot milk
1 pkg. lemon pudding, prepared
coconut

Beat eggs until light and fluffy, about 10 minutes. Slowly add sugar and beat. Add flour, baking powder and vanila on top of mixture. Add 1 cup hot milk all at once; fold in hot milk and dry ingredients within one minute. Bake in ungreased 9x13 pan for 30 minutes at 350 degrees. Let stand a few minutes, then run knife around edges and spatula underneath to loosen cake. Turn over onto cookie sheet. Cut into 2 layers using long serrated knife. Put bottom back in pan. Frost with half of the cooked lemon pudding. Top with other half of cake and frost with remaining pudding. Sprinkle with coconut.

Lazy Daisy Oatmeal Cake

1 1/4 cups boiling water
1 cup oatmeal, uncooked
1/2 cup butter or margarine
1 cup granulated sugar
1 cup firmly packed brown sugar
1 tsp. vanilla

2 eggs
1 1/2 cups flour
1 tsp. soda
1/2 tsp. salt
3/4 tsp. cinnamon
1/4 tsp. nutmeg

Pour boiling water over oats; cover and let stand 20 minutes. Beat butter until creamy; gradually add sugars and beat until fluffy. Blend in vanilla and eggs. Add oats mixture; mix well. Blend together flour, soda, salt, cinnamon, and nutmeg. Add to creamed mixture. Mix well. Pour batter into well-greased and floured 9-inch square pan. Bake 50-55 minutes at 350 degrees. Do not remove cake from pan. Frost with Lazy Daisy Frosting.

Creme De Menthe Bundt Cake

1 pkg. yellow cake mix
1 pkg. pistachio instant pudding mix
3 Tbsp. creme de mente and enough
    water to make 1 cup

1 cup oil
4 eggs
few drops of green food coloring

Mix all ingredients together. Place 2/3 of the batter in well greased bundt pan. Add 1/4 cup chocolate syrup to remaining batter; mix well. Pour over green batter. Marble with a knife. Bake at 350 degrees for 1 hour. Cool for 20 minutes. Meanwhile, to make frosting, combine 1/2 cup sugar, 2 Tbsp. butter and 2 Tbsp. milk; boil 1 minute. Take off heat and add 6 oz. chocolate chips. Drizzle over cooled cake.

Red Velvet Cake

1 1/2 cup sugar
1 cup butter
2 eggs
2 oz. red food coloring
1 tsp. vanilla

2 1/2 cups cake flour
2 Tbsp. cocoa
1 cup buttermilk
1 tsp. soda
1 tsp. vinegar

Cream sugar and butter. Add eggs, one at a time, beating after each egg. Add red food coloring and vanilla. Mix in flour, cocoa, and buttermilk, alternating flour/cocoa and buttermilk when mixing. Mix the soda and vinegar in small container and add to cake mixture. Bake in <u>three</u> 8 or 9-inch round layer pans at 350 degrees for 25 minutes. Frost with Red Velvet Cake Frosting.

Watergate Cake

1 white cake mix
2 boxes pistachio instant pudding
1 cup vegetable oil
3 eggs

1 cup 7-Up
1/2 cup nuts
1 1/4 cups cold milk
8 oz. Cool Whip

Combine cake mix, 1 box pistachio instant pudding, oil, eggs, 7-Up and nuts. Mix well and pour into greased 9x13-inch cake pan. Bake at 350 degrees for 30-35 minutes. Cool. Add cold milk to remaining box of pudding mix; whip until thick. Fold in Cool Whip. Frost cake. Keep in refrigerator. Garnish with chopped nuts, if desired.

Caramel Frosting

1/2 cup brown sugar
1/2 cup white sugar

1/4 cup milk
1/4 cup butter

Cook all ingredients together for 2 minutes. Beat until of spreading consistency.

Lazy Daisy Frosting

1/2 cup butter, melted
1 cup firmly packed brown sugar
6 Tbsp. cream

1 1/2 cups shredded coconut
2/3 cup chopped nuts (optional)

Combine ingredients. Spread on warm cake; place under broiler until slightly browned.

Coconut Cream Cheese Frosting

4 Tbsp. butter or margarine
2 cups flake coconut
8 oz. cream cheese, softened

2 tsp. milk
3 1/2 cups powdered sugar
1/2 tsp. vanilla

Melt 2 Tbsp. butter in skillet. Add coconut; stir constantly over low heat until golden brown. Spread coconut on absorbent paper to cool. Cream 2 Tbsp. butter with cream cheese. Add milk and sugar alternately, beating well. Add vanilla; stir in 1 3/4 cups of the coconut. Makes enough to spread on tops and sides of layer cake. Sprinkle with remaining coconut. Great with Coconut Cake.

Chocolate Cream Cheese Frosting

4 oz. German sweet chocolate
1 1/2 Tbsp. water
3 oz. softened cream cheese

1 1/2 cups confectioners' sugar
1/4 tsp. salt
1/2 tsp. vanilla

Heat chocolate with water over very low heat, stirring constantly, until chocolate is melted. Remove from heat; cool until lukewarm. Add cream cheese and stir until well blended. Stir in powdered sugar, then add salt and vanilla. Let stand a few minutes until it reaches right consistency for spreading.

Cream Cheese Frosting

6 oz. cream cheese, softened
6 Tbsp. butter
1 tsp. vanilla

1 Tbsp. crean
4 cups powde

Mix together cream cheese, margarine, vanilla and cream. S
correct consistency.

Brown Beauty Icing

1 1/3 cups confectioners' sugar
1/4 cup shortening
1/4 cup milk

3 oz.unsweetened chocolate, melted
1 tsp. vanilla
1 whole egg (or 3 egg yolks)

Blend sugar, shortening, milk, chocolate and vanilla in mixing bowl. Add egg. Beat with
rotary beater just until frosting is smooth. Place bowl in ice water and stir until frosting is
thick enough to spread. If frosting becomes too thick, dip bowl in hot water for a few
seconds and stir to desired consistency. Makes frosting for two 8 or 9" layers or 9x13"
oblong.

Easy Creamy Chocolate Frosting

1/4 cup boiling water
2 Tbsp. butter
2 squares chocolate

2 cups powdered sugar
1 tsp. vanilla

Place water, butter and chocolate in saucepan. Heat until chocolate is melted and appears
curdled. Remove from heat and add sugar. Beat until right consistency for spreading.
Add vanilla.

Chocolate Brownie Frosting

1/2 cup butter
1 1/2 cups sugar
6 Tbsp. milk

2 cups miniature marshmallows
1/2 cup chocolate chips

Combine butter, sugar and milk in saucepan and bring to a boil for 2 minutes. Remove
from heat and stir in miniature marshmallows and chocolate chips; stir until melted. Spread
on brownies.

ocolate Frosting

p butter
uares unsweetened chocolate
1/2 cups brown sugar, packed

1/2 cup milk
1 1/2 cups powdered sugar

Melt butter with chocolate. Blend in brown sugar and milk. Cook and stir to a boil; simmer 4 minutes, stirring occasionally. Remove from heat. Beat in powdered sugar. Cool, beating occasionally until thick enough to spread. (Note: If frosting stiffens, add about 1 teaspoon hot water.)

EZ Frosting

1/2 cup butter
1 egg yolk
2 Tbsp. milk

1/2 tsp. vanilla
2 to 3 cups powdered sugar

Combine all ingredients except powdered sugar. Stir together; add powdered sugar and blend until of spreading consistency.

Easy Creamy Frosting

1 small pkg. instant pudding mix, any flavor
1/4 cup powdered sugar

1 cup cold milk
8 oz. Cool Whip

Combine the pudding mix, powdered sugar and milk in small bowl; beat slowly with rotary beater or lowest speed of electric mixer until well blended, about 1 minute. Fold in Cool Whip. Makes enough frosting for 9x13 cake or two 9-inch layers. Store frosted cake in refrigerator.

Caramel Frosting

1/2 cup butter or margarine
1 1/2 cups firmly packed brown sugar

1/3 cup milk
4 cups powdered sugar

Melt butter in saucepan; stir in brown sugar. Cook over low heat 2 minutes. Add milk; bring to a full boil. Cool to lukewarm without stirring. Add powdered sugar; beat until of spreading consistency. Thin with milk, if necessary.

Red Velvet Cake Frosting

1 cup milk
2 Tbsp. flour
1 tsp. vanilla

1 cup sugar
1 cup butter

Cook milk and flour in double boiler. Cool. Beat sugar and butter until fluffy. Add cream mixture and beat again until fluffy. Add vanilla and mix. Makes enough to frost three-layer Red Velvet Cake.

Ivory Satin Frosting

1/2 cup sugar
1/4 cup firmly packed brown sugar
1/4 cup light corn syrup
2 egg whites

2 Tbsp. water
1/4 tsp. cream of tartar
1/8 tsp. salt
1/2 tsp. vanilla

Combine all ingredients, except vanilla, in top of double boiler. Cook over boiling water, beating constantly until mixture stands in peaks. Remove from heat. Add vanilla; beat until of spreading consistency.

Fluffy White 7-Minute Frosting

1 cup sugar
1/3 cup water
2 unbeaten egg whites

1 tsp. vanilla
1/4 tsp. cream of tartar
dash salt

Combine sugar, water, cream of tartar and salt in saucepan. Bring to boiling, stirring until sugar dissolves. Very slowly add to unbeaten egg whites in bowl, beating constantly with mixer until stiff peaks form. Beat in vanilla. Will frost a 9x13 cake.

Dessert Icing

1 egg white
1/2 tsp. cinnamon
1/2 cup white sugar

1/2 tsp. cream of tartar
1/4 cup boiling water

Beat egg white and cream of tartar until foamy. Gradually add sugar while beating and beat until stiff peaks form. Add boiling water slowly while beating. Beat until stiff peaks form. Add cinnamon or jam of choice (about 3 Tbsp.)

Decorator's Icing

1 tsp. vanilla (or almond extract)
3/4 cup margarine
3/4 cup shortening, like Crisco

1/2 cup water
2 1/2 lbs. powdered sugar

Mix well together. Can be colored with food coloring.

Thin Glaze

1 1/2 Tbsp. water
2 cups sifted confectioners' sugar

2 1/2 Tbsp. white corn syrup
1 tsp. flavoring

Combine all ingredients and drizzle over cake.

Butterscotch Sauce

1/2 cup white sugar
1/2 cup brown sugar

1/4 cup butter
1/2 cup whipping cream

Combine all ingredients; bring to boil until of proper consistency, stirring constantly.
Serve warm over cake. Great with Apple Cake.

Orange Butter Icing

2 1/2 Tbsp. soft butter or margarine
1 1/2 cups powdered sugar

1 1/2 Tbsp. orange juice
2 tsp. grated orange rind

Blend butter and sugar together. Stir in orange juice and rind until smooth. Makes icing
for 4 dozen cookies. Great with Orange Drop Cookies.

Lemon Frosting

3/4 cup powdered sugar
1 Tbsp. margarine

1 tsp. vanilla
1 1/2 tsp. lemon juice

Blend all ingrdients and spread on bars. Refrigerate before cutting into bars.   Enough for
8 inch square pan of bars.

Brown Sugar Filling for Layer Cakes

1 cup brown sugar
1 Tbsp. corn starch

1 cup sour cream
2 or more egg yolks

Combine all ingredients in saucepan and cook until it thickens. Put this between two cake layers. Then frost with Angel Icing.

Angel Icing

1 egg white
1 cup sugar
1 Tbsp. light corn syrup

1/4 cup water
1 tsp. vanilla

Beat egg white until stiff. Boil sugar, corn syrup and water to hard ball stage or until it threads. Pour hot syrup into beaten egg white. Continue beating until mixture will hold a peak when beater is raised. Add vanilla and spread on cake.

PAGEANTS

I still watch the Miss America Pageant every September, just like when I was a young girl. I used to dream of being on stage, receiving a crown and flowers, and walking down a long runway. I just assumed it was a dream and could never become reality.

When I was a junior in high school, our little town decided to have a Miss Liberty Belle Pageant in 1976, so I entered. There were 13 girls competing and to my surprise, I won. My two brothers immediately started calling me "Miss Ding Dong." Brothers can be that way! That pageant led to competing at the county level two months later and, after winning, going on to a state competition called Miss Teenage Minnesota. I didn't even get in the top ten, so I left saying, "I'll never do that again." (Famous last words!) Within eight months, I was competing for another state title, Miss Minnesota United Teenager. I had better results this time - I won. Even though I went to the national competition in Washington, D.C., and did not win there, it was this pageant that became a very important part of my life. By the following year, I was emceeing teen pageants in Minnesota and other states, and ended up doing this for the next fourteen years. One summer, I emceed as many as 25 of the 50 state pageants for the MISS T.E.E.N. Pageant. I was asked to emcee their National Pageant, and did that for the next six years. It was a true highlight each year. It was such fun to meet the "cream of the crop" of excellent young women, teach the choreography, and sing and entertain the audience.

I had just turned 30 when Mark said, "Why don't you try for the title of Mrs. Minnesota?" Being a fairly competitive person, I took it on as a challenge to myself to lose some weight, get in shape and to get all the work done to be prepared to compete. Eric was only one-and-a-half years old and I was working full-time at CVN, so it was a hectic time. But, all the work paid off, and I won. I really enjoyed speaking to various groups, riding in parades, and CVN even put up a billboard for me. It's wild to be driving down the road and there you are...bigger than life! I nearly drove off the road the first time I saw it! I spent two weeks in Las Vegas in March, 1990, competing in the Mrs. America Pageant. It was two weeks of rehearsals and video tapings, since it was televised nationwide. I didn't win, but it was a thrill to be on the stage with all the other married women from around the country.

So many people ask me, "Why be in pageants?" For me, it was always an opportunity to better myself, to improve my interviewing skills and to take on the challenge of very hard work and achieving a goal. You learn a lot about yourself along the way. You win some and you lose some, but the satisfaction comes in knowing that you did the best you could and being happy with that. It broadened my horizons, took me to places I'd never been, introduced me to some wonderful people and allowed me experiences I would not have had otherwise.

Miss Liberty Belle

Miss Minnesota United Teenager

Visiting the Miss America Pageant (above)
with my good friend, Gretchen Carlson,
Miss America, 1989 (below)

Mistress of Ceremonies
for the MISS T.E.E.N. Pageant

CVN put up this billboard.

**MRS.
MINNESOTA
1989**

Cookies, Bars & Candies

Cherry Delights

1 cup butter or margarine
1/2 cup sugar
1/2 cup light corn syrup
2 eggs, separated into yolks and whites

2 1/2 cups flour
2 cups finely chopped nuts
candied cherry halves

Combine butter and sugar. Beat until light and fluffy. Add corn syrup, egg yolks and flour. Mix well and chill. Lightly beat the egg whites. Shape dough into 1 inch balls. Dip each in egg whites and coat with chopped nuts. Press candied cherry halves, cut side down, into center of each cookie. Place cookies about an inch-and-a-half apart on greased baking sheets. Bake at 325 degrees for 20 minutes. Makes 4 dozen.

Apricot Twists

2 cups flour
8 oz. cream cheese

1 cup butter
apricot jam

Mix together flour, cream cheese and butter. Roll out about 1/4" thick and cut off edges to make rectangle about 9" high. Spread with apricot jam. Fold into thirds and cut into strips 1/2 to 3/4 inches wide. Twist each strip 1/2 turn as you put them on a greased cookie sheet. Bake at 350 degrees for 15-16 minutes. While still warm, coat with powdered sugar.

Applesauce Cookies

3/4 cup soft shortening
1 cup brown sugar, packed
1 egg
1/2 cup applesauce
2 1/4 cups flour
1/2 tsp. soda

1/2 tsp. salt
3/4 tsp. cinnamon
1/4 tsp. cloves
1 cup seedless raisins
1/2 cup chopped nuts

Heat oven to 375 degrees. Mix shortening, sugar and egg thoroughly. Stir in applesauce. Blend dry ingredients; stir in. Mix in raisins and nuts. Drop by teaspoonfuls onto greased baking sheet. Bake 10 to 12 minutes. Makes 4 dozen cookies.

Orange Drop Cookies

2/3 cup shortening
3/4 cup sugar
1 egg
1/2 cup orange juice
2 Tbsp. grated orange rind

2 cups flour
1/2 tsp. baking powder
1/2 tsp. soda
1/2 tsp. salt

Heat oven to 400 degrees. Mix shortening, sugar, and egg thoroughly. Stir in orange juice and rind. Blend in dry ingredients. Drop by rounded teaspoonfuls, about 2 inches apart, on ungreased baking sheet. Bake 8 to 10 minutes or until delicately browned on edges. Frost with Orange Butter Icing.

Banana Spice Cookies

1/2 cup soft shortening
1 cup brown sugar, packed
2 eggs
1 cup mashed bananas
2 cups flour
2 tsp. baking powder

1/4 tsp. soda
1/4 tsp. salt
1/2 tsp. cinnamon
1/4 tsp. cloves
1/2 cup chopped nuts

Mix well shortening, sugar and eggs. Stir in bananas. Mix dry ingredients and stir in. Blend in nuts. Chill about 1 hour. Heat oven to 375 degrees . Drop by rounded tablespoonfuls 2" apart on lightly greased baking sheet. Bake 8 to 10 minutes. Frost with powdered sugar frosting. Makes 3 to 4 dozen cookies.

Almond Cookies

1 cup butter
1/2 cup sugar
1 2/3 cups flour

1 cup almonds, chopped fine
2 tsp. vanilla

Cream butter and sugar; add flour, almonds, and vanilla. Roll out 1/8" thick and cut with a cookie cutter. Bake for 15 minutes in a 300 degree oven. Dip in granulated sugar while still warm.

Pecan Cookies

2 cups flour
1 cup butter
1/4 cup white sugar

2 tsp. vanilla
pecans

Mix flour, butter, sugar and vanilla as for pie crust. Pinch off dough about the size of a walnut and wrap around 1/2 pecan. Place on cookie sheet. Bake 10 minutes at 350 degrees. While still hot, roll in powdered sugar.

Walnut Butter Balls

1 cup butter or margarine
1 cup brown sugar
1 egg

1 tsp. vanilla
2 cups flour
walnuts

Cream together the butter, brown sugar and egg; add vanilla and flour and mix well. Roll dough in balls, the size of a walnut. Roll in sugar and place on cookie sheet, pressing down slightly. Place one walnut on top of each cookie. Bake at 375 for 10-12 minutes or until golden brown.

Jodekager II

1 cup sugar
1 1/2 cups butter
2 eggs

4 cups flour
1 tsp. vanilla
1 tsp. carbonated ammonia

Cream butter and sugar; add eggs and flavoring. Add flour and ammonia which has been dissolved in a small amount of water. Knead well. Roll thin and cut with cookie cutter. Sprinkle with sugar before baking at 375 degrees until brown around the edges.

No Bake Cookies

2 cups sugar
1/3 cup cocoa
1/2 cup butter or margarine
1/4 cup milk

1/3 cup peanut butter
2 cups quick oats
1 tsp. vanilla
3/4 cup chopped nuts

Combine ingredients and drop by teaspoonfuls onto waxed paper.

Crisp Unusual Cookies

1 cup margarine
2 cups sugar
2 eggs
1 tsp. vanilla
1 cup vegetable oil

5 cups flour
1/2 tsp. salt
2 tsp. baking soda
2 tsp. cream of tartar

Cream margarine and sugar. Add eggs and beat. Add remaining ingredients and mix. Roll dough in small balls, dip in sugar, put on cookie sheet and press down with fork. Bake at 350 degrees until golden brown.

Crinkles

1 German chocolate cake mix
1/2 cup instant potato flakes
1 egg
1 tsp. cream of tartar
1 tsp. cinnamon

3 Tbsp. milk
3/4 cup melted butter
1/2 cup chopped nuts
1/2 cup sugar

Heat oven to 350 degrees. Combine all ingredients except nuts and sugar; blend well. Stir in nuts. Let stand 5 minutes. Drop by spoonfuls into sugar to coat and place on cookie sheets. Bake for 10 minutes. Frost with mixture of 1 cup powdered sugar, 2 tsp. unsweetened cocoa, 1 Tbsp. soft butter and 1 to 2 Tbsp. milk.

Pheffernuts

10 cups flour
1 cup sugar
3 cups light corn syrup
1 tsp. soda

2 tsp. cinnamon
2 tsp. cloves
2 tsp. allspice
1 cup lard

Combine all ingredients; mix well. Roll out thin and cut into two-inch squares. Place on cookie sheet and bake at 350 degrees for 8-10 minutes or until lightly browned.

Coconut Balls

2 lbs. confectioners' sugar
14 oz. can sweetened condensed milk
1/2 cup margarine
8 to 12 oz. flaked coconut

pinch salt
1/2 cup chopped pecans
12 oz. chocolate chips
2 Tbsp. parafin wax

Melt butter and add milk. Stir in sugar and salt. Add coconut and pecans; chill, then roll into balls. Insert a toothpick into each ball and freeze. Melt chocolate chips and parafin in double boiler. Dip each ball in chocolate mixture and set on waxed paper.

Tea Cakes

1 cup butter
1/2 cup powdered sugar
1 tsp. vanilla

2 1/2 cups flour
1/4 tsp. salt
3/4 cup chopped nuts

Cream butter, powdered sugar and vanilla. Add remaining ingredients. Roll into 1-inch balls. Bake at 350 degrees on ungreased cookie sheet until set, but not brown. While warm, roll in powdered sugar; cool and roll again.

"Jim Dandy" Cookies

1 1/2 cups flour
1/2 tsp. soda
1/2 tsp. salt
2/3 cup brown sugar, firmly packed
1/2 cup shortening
1 egg

1/4 cup maraschino cherry juice
2 Tbsp. milk
2 oz. squares unsweetened chocolate
1/2 cup chopped nuts
1/4 cup Maraschino cherries, cut up
large marshmallows, cut in half

Combine flour, soda and salt. Cream brown sugar and shortening. Blend in unbeaten egg. Stir in half of dry ingredients. Add cherry juice and milk. Mix well. Blend in 2 squares melted unsweetened chocolate, the rest of the dry ingredients and then the chopped nuts and chopped cherries. Drop by rounded teaspoonfuls onto ungreased cookie sheet. Bake at 350 degrees for 12 to 15 minutes. When cookies are done, place a half marshmallow on top of each, cut side down, and put back into the oven for a few seconds, until you can flatten the marshmallow a bit with a fork. When cool, frost with chocolate frosting and top with a nut half or chopped nuts.
Frosting: In top of double boiler, over boiling water, cook 1/2 cup milk, 1/4 cup butter or margarine, 2 squares unsweetened chocolate and 1/8 tsp. salt; cook until thick, stirring constantly. Remove from heat. Stir in 1 tsp. vanilla and 2 to 2 1/2 cups powdered sugar, until of spreading consistency. (Can use mixer for this.)

Minnesota Mint Snowballs

1 cup shortening
1/2 cup powdered sugar
2 tsp. water
1/2 tsp. salt
2 cups sifted flour
1 cup quick oatmeal

2 cups powdered sugar
1/2 tsp. mint extract
1/4 cup milk
green food coloring
shredded coconut

Mix together the shortening, 1/2 cup powdered sugar, water, salt, flour and oatmeal. Roll into small balls and place on cookie sheet. Bake 25 to 30 minutes at 350 degrees. Mix together 2 cups powdered sugar, mint extract, milk and green food coloring. Dip balls in frosting and roll in shredded coconut.

Spritz Cookie Sticks

1 cup butter or margarine
3/4 cup sugar
1 tsp. vanilla

1/4 tsp. salt
1 egg
2 1/4 cups flour

Cream together all ingredients except flour. Blend in flour. Divide dough in half. Spread each half with floured fingers or spatula to a 12x10-inch rectangle on ungreased cookie sheet. Run floured fork tines over top to make "spritz" marks. Sprinkle with colored sugars, if desired. Bake at 350 degrees for 15 to 20 minutes, or until delicately browned. Cut immediately into 3x1-inch sticks. Remove from cookie sheet. Makes 72 cookies. To make chocolate cookies, increase sugar to 1 cup and add 2 ounces melted unsweetened chocolate. Do not overbake. To make Pepperkakor "Spritz," omit egg, add 1/4 cup light molasses and 1/2 tsp. each of cinnamon, nutmeg, cloves and ginger.

Ranch House Cookies

2 cups brown sugar
1 cup granulated sugar
2 cups shortening
1 cup raisins
2 tsp. baking soda

3 1/2 cups flour (or more)
4 eggs
2 cups quick oats
1 cup coconut
2 cups cornflakes, crushed a little

Cream together the shortening and sugars; add remaining ingredients and mix well. Make into small balls; put on cookie sheet and flatten a little. Bake in 350 degree oven about 10 minutes.

Chow Mein Cookies

1 cup peanut butter   *4 cups miniature marshmallows*
12 oz. butterscotch chips   *4 cups chow mein noodles*

Place peanut butter and butterscotch chips in top of double boiler. Heat over hot water until melted. Combine with marshmallows and chow mein noodles. Mix well and drop by spoonfuls onto waxed paper. Chill.

Ghosties

1/2 tsp. salt   *3 cups corn flakes*
3 egg whites   *1 cup semi-sweet chocolate chips*
3/4 cup sugar   *1 tsp. vanilla*

Add salt to egg whites; beat until stiff. Gradually add sugar; beat very stiff. Fold in remaining ingredients. Drop by teaspoonfuls onto greased cookie sheet. Bake at 350 degrees for 15 minutes or until done. Makes 30 cookies.

Coconut Refrigerator Cookies

1 cup brown sugar   *2 eggs*
1 cup white sugar   *3 cups flour*
1 cup butter or margarine   *2 cups coconut*
1 tsp. baking soda

Cream together sugars, butter and eggs. Add remaining ingredients. Roll dough into small rolls and place on waxed paper in refrigerator. When chilled, slice thin and place on cookie sheet. Bake at 375 degrees for 8 to 10 minutes.

Sugar Cookies

2 eggs
2/3 cup oil
2 tsp. vanilla
3/4 cup sugar

1/4 cup butter
2 cups flour
2 tsp. baking powder
1/2 tsp. salt

Beat the eggs with a fork; stir in the oil and vanilla. Blend in the sugar and butter until mixture thickens. Stir in the flour, baking powder and salt. Drop by teaspoonfuls on ungreased cookie sheet. Flatten with bottom of glass, greased and dipped in sugar. Bake 8 to 10 minutes at 400 degrees until delicate brown.

World's Best Sugar Cookies

1 cup powdered sugar
1 cup granulated sugar
1 cup butter
1 cup vegetable oil
2 eggs, beaten

2 tsp. vanilla
5 cups flour
1 tsp. baking soda
1 tsp. cream of tartar
1/4 tsp. salt

Cream together sugars and butter. Add remaining ingredients and mix well. Roll into small balls. Press with cookie press or fancy glass bottom dipped in sugar. Sprinkle sugar generously on top. Bake in 350 degree oven for 10 to 12 minutes.

Forgotten Cookies

2 egg whites
2/3 cup sugar
1 cup chocolate chips

1 cup chopped pecans
pinch of salt

Heat oven to 350 degrees. Beat egg whites until foamy and thick. Gradually add sugar; beat until stiff. Add chocolate chips, chopped nuts and salt. Drop by teaspoonsful in small peaks on foil-lined cookie sheets. Place in preheated oven. Turn off heat. Leave overnight. Makes 2 dozen.

Christmas Wreaths

1/2 cup butter or margarine
30 marshmallows
green food coloring

1/2 tsp. vanilla
1/4 tsp. salt
3 1/2 cups corn flakes

Melt the butter and marshmallows over low heat. Add green food coloring to marshmallow mixture to make it very green. Add remaining ingredients and blend. While still warm, drop by heaping tablespoonfuls onto waxed paper and form into wreaths. (Dip your fingertips in a bowl of cold water before forming each wreath to prevent sticking.) Decorate with red hots (candy) to appear as a Christmas wreath.

Hi Ho Cookies

Hi Ho Crackers
1 1/2 lbs. almond bark

peanut butter
12 oz. chocolate chips

Spread peanut butter on Hi Ho crackers. Top with second cracker; about 80 sandwiches. Melt almond bark with chocolate chips. Dip sandwich cookies into the chocolate mixture and let cool.

Chocolate Bon Bons

1 cup ground nuts
1/2 cup soft butter
1 cup peanut butter
1 tsp. vanilla

2 cups powdered sugar
12 oz. chocolate chips
2 Tbsp. parafin wax

Combine nuts, butter, peanut butter, vanilla, and powdered sugar. Stir by hand and shape into balls. Dip into melted chocolate chips and parafin wax mixed together. Use fork to coat and drop on waxed paper.

Brownie Chip Cookies

1 pkg. fudge brownie mix   1/4 cup oil
2 eggs   1 cup chocolate chips

Grease cookie sheet. In large bowl, combine brownie mix, eggs and oil. Beat with spoon about 50 strokes. Stir in chocolate chips. Drop by rounded teaspoonfuls, 2 inches apart, onto cookie sheets. Bake at 350 degrees for 8-10 minutes. Cookies are soft to the touch. Cool slightly before removing from cookie sheets. If desired, frost. (Note: Dough may be very crumbly.)

Grandma Beldin Cookies

2 cups sugar   1/4 cup butter
1/2 cup milk   1 tsp. vanilla
6 Tbsp. cocoa   2 cups quick rolled oats

Combine sugar, milk and cocoa; cook for 3 minutes. Add butter and vanilla; cool 20 minutes. Add rolled oats. Drop by spoonfuls on wax paper.

Chocolate Chip Rice Krispie Cookies

1 cup brown sugar   1 tsp. cream of tartar
1 cup white sugar   1 tsp. salt
1 cup salad oil   3 1/2 cups flour
1 cup margarine   1 cup coconut
1 egg   1 cup Rice Krispies
2 tsp. vanilla   1 cup oatmeal
1 tsp. soda   12 oz. chocolate chips

Mix together sugars, salad oil, margarine, egg and vanilla. Add remaining ingredients and mix well. Drop by teaspoonfuls onto cookie sheet. Bake at 350 degrees for 10-12 minutes.

Monster Cookies

1 dozen eggs	3 lbs. peanut butter
1 lb. margarine	1 Tbsp. corn syrup
2 lbs. brown sugar	1 Tbsp. vanilla
4 cups white sugar	1 lb. M & M's
18 cups oatmeal	1 lb. chocolate chips
8 Tbsp. baking soda	

Combine eggs, margarine, peanut butter, corn syrup and vanilla; beat well. Beat in the sugars, using mixer for this. Stir in remaining ingredients. Shape with small ice cream scoop and put on greased cookie sheet; flatten slightly. Bake at 350 degrees for 10-12 minutes. Let cool slightly before removing from pan.

Chocolate Chip Yummies

2 cups butter	4 tsp. vanilla
2 cups powdered sugar	2 cups Quick oatmeal
3 cups flour	1 pkg. chocolate chips
1 tsp. soda	

Cream butter and sugar; add soda and flour, mixing well. Add vanilla, oatmeal and chocolate chips. Form into small balls and press with a fork. Bake for 12-15 minutes in a 325 degree oven. Makes about 11 dozen cookies.

Chocolate Chip Meringues

2 egg whites	1 cup coconut
1 cup powdered sugar	2 cups corn flakes
1/2 tsp. vanilla	6 oz. chocolate chips
1/4 tsp. salt	

Beat egg whites until soft peaks form. Add sugar 1/2 cup at a time. Beat well after each addition. Beat in vanilla and salt. Fold in coconut, corn flakes and chocolate chips. Drop by teaspoonfuls onto greased pan. Bake at 300 degrees for 20-25 minutes.

Peanut Blossoms

1 3/4 cups sifted flour
1 tsp. soda
1/2 tsp. salt
1/2 cup butter
1/2 cup peanut butter

1/2 cup sugar
1/2 cup brown sugar, packed
1 egg
1 tsp. vanilla
36 solid milk chocolate candy kisses

Blend together flour, soda and salt. Cream together the butter and peanut butter. Gradually add the sugar and brown sugar, creaming well. Add 1 egg and vanilla. Beat well. Blend in the dry ingredients; mix thoroughly. Shape dough into balls, using a rounded teaspoonful for each. Roll balls in sugar and place on ungreased cookie sheet. Bake at 375 degrees for 8 minutes. Remove sheet from oven and place a chocolate candy kiss on top of each cookie, pressing down firmly so that cookie cracks around the edge. Return cookies to oven and bake 2 to 5 minutes longer until golden brown. Makes about 3 dozen cookies.

Chocolate Oatmeal Drop Cookies

3 cups quick oats
1/2 cup chopped nuts
1/2 cup coconut
2 cups white sugar

3 heaping Tbsp. cocoa
pinch of slat
1/2 cup butter or solid shortening
1/2 cup milk

Combine oats, nuts and coconut; set aside. Combine remaining ingredients in saucepan and bring to full boil; boil for one minute. Dump oats, nuts and coconut into cooked mixture and drop by teaspoonfuls onto waxed paper. Let cool.

Peanut Butter Cookies

1 cup butter
1 cup brown sugar
1 cup white sugar
2 eggs

1 cup peanut butter
2 1/2 cups flour
2 tsp. baking soda
1 tsp. vanilla

Cream butter and sugars; add eggs, vanilla and peanut butter and mix well. Mix in dry ingredients. Let dough stand 15 minutes. Roll into balls the size of walnuts. Place 3" apart on lightly greased baking sheet. With flour dipped fork, flatten dough criss-cross fashion to 3-4 inches in diameter. Bake at 375 degrees for 10 to 12 minutes or until lgihtly browned. Let cool slightly before removing from baking sheet.

Unbelievable Peanut Butter Cookies

1 cup peanut butter
1 cup sugar
3 Tbsp. butter

1 egg, unbeaten
bag of chocolate stars

Mix all ingredients together, except chocolate stars. Drop by teaspoonfuls onto greased cookie sheet. Press with fork in both directions across the top of the cookie. Bake at 350 degrees for 8 minutes or until light brown. Place chocolate star in center of each cookie immediately after removing from oven. Makes 24 cookies.

Melt Aways

1 cup butter
1/2 cup powdered sugar
3/4 cup corn starch
1 cup flour
1/2 tsp. grated lemon or orange rind

4 Tbsp. butter
2 cups powdered sugar
2 tsp. lemon juice or 2 Tbsp. orange juice
milk, if needed

Cream the first two ingredients; add the next three ingredients and mix well. Chill for 1 hour and then shape into small balls. Put on a greased cookie sheet and press lightly. Bake at 350 degrees 15-20 minutes (do not brown). Frost with remaining ingredients mixed.

Almond Bark Cookies

1 pkg. almond bark coating
2 cups Rice Krispies
2 cups corn flakes

3 cups miniature marshmallows
2 cups chopped walnuts
1 cup coconut

Melt almond bark in 6 quart kettle (T-Fal works great!) or roaster in oven at 200 degrees. When melted, mix all ingredients together and drop on wax paper. These balls freeze well.

Oatmeal Cookies

1 cup butter	1 tso. vanilla
scant 1/2 cup lard	1 1/2 tsp. baking soda
1 cup brown sugar	1 1/2 tsp. hot water
1 cup white sugar	2 1/3 cup oatmeal
1 tsp. salt	2 1/2 flour
2 eggs	1/2 cup nuts

Cream butter, shortening and sugars. Add eggs, salt and vanilla. Mix well. Add remaining ingredients and blend. Drop by teaspoonfuls onto cookie sheet. Bake at 375 degrees for 8 to 10 minutes.

Oatmeal Butterscotch Cookies

1 cup shortening	1 tsp. soda
3/4 cup brown sugar	1 1/2 cups flour
3/4 cup white sugar	1 pkg. butterscotch chips
2 eggs, beaten	2 cups oatmeal
1 Tbsp. hot water	1/2 cup chopped nuts
1 tsp. vanilla	

Mix above ingredients in order given. Drop by teaspoonfuls onto cookie sheet. Bake at 375 degrees for 10 minutes.

Butterscotch Cookies

1/2 cup butter	1/2 tsp. salt
1 1/2 cups dark brown sugar	1 cup sour cream or 1 cup evaporated
2 eggs	milk mixed with 1 Tbsp. vinegar
1 tsp. vanilla	2 1/2 cups flour
1 tsp. baking soda	2/3 cup chopped nuts
1/2 tsp. baking powder	

Cream butter and sugar. Add eggs and vanilla and beat well. Add sour cream. Combine dry ingredients and add to creamed mixture, mixing just to combine. Add nuts. Drop by teaspoonfuls onto greased cookie sheet and bake at 350 degrees for 10 minutes. Cool and frost. Frosting: 1/4 cup butter, melted and browned; 2 cups powdered sugar; 3 Tbsp. boiling water; 1 tsp. vanilla. Mix to spreading consistency; spread while frosting is warm.

Easiest & Best Brownies

2 cups sugar
1/2 cup cocoa
1 cup melted butter
4 eggs

2 tsp. vanilla
1 1/2 cups flour
3/4 tsp. salt

Mix together and bake at 350 degrees for 25 minutes.

FROSTING: Boil together for one minute: 6 Tbsp. milk, 1/2 cup butter, and 1 1/2 cups sugar. Remove from heat. Add 1/2 cup chocolate chips, stirring until melted. Pour on cooled brownies.

Mom's Brownies

3 squares chocolate
1 cup butter
2 cups sugar
4 eggs

1 cup flour
2 tsp. vanilla
chopped nuts (optional)

Melt chocolate and set aside. Cream butter and sugar. Add eggs and beat well. Add chocolate and flour. Mix well. Add vanilla and nuts, if desired. Bake 40 minutes at 350 degrees.

Marble Brownies

any brownie recipe
6 oz. cream cheese, softened
8 Tbsp. butter
1/3 cup sugar
2 eggs

2 Tbsp. flour
1 3/4 tsp. vanilla
2 Tbsp. cocoa
1 1/2 cups powdered sugar
2 Tbsp. milk

Make any brownie recipe. Spread 1/2 of the mixture in a greased 9x13 pan. Combine cream cheese and 5 Tbsp. butter; beat together. Add sugar, eggs, flour and 3/4 tsp. vanilla. Beat until smooth. Pour cream cheese mixture over brownie mix in pan. Drop remaining brownie mixture by spoonfuls over cheese mixture. Zigzag a knife through batter to marble. Bake according to brownie directions. To frost, melt 3 Tbsp. butter, stir in cocoa until dissolved. Add powdered sugar, milk and 1 tsp. vanilla.

Meltaway Brownies

any brownie recipe
1/2 cup chopped nuts
1/2 cup flake coconut
3 cups powdered sugar
1/3 cup margarine or butter, melted

1 1/2 tsp. vanilla
2 Tbsp. milk
2 oz. squares unsweetened chocolate
2 tsp. margarine or butter

Heat oven to 350 degrees. Prepare brownies according to recipe, except stir coconut and nuts into dough; bake as directed and cool. Mix powdered sugar, 1/3 cup margarine and the vanilla. Stir in milk, 1 tsp. at a time, until of spreading consistency; spread over brownies. Refrigerate until topping is firm, about 30 minutes. Heat chocolate and 2 tsp. margarine until melted. Drizzle evenly over topping; spread evenly. Refrigerate until chocolate is firm, about 15 minutes. Store in refrigerator.

Golden Peanut Butter Brownies

2 1/4 cups flour
2 1/2 tsp. baking powder
1/2 tsp. salt
2/3 cup butter, softened
2/3 cup smooth peanut butter

1 1/4 cups white sugar
1 1/4 cups brown sugar, firmly packed
1 tsp. vanilla extract
3 eggs
12 oz. chocolate chips

Preheat oven to 350 degrees. In small bowl, combine flour, baking powder and salt; set aside. In large bowl, combine butter, peanut butter, sugar, brown sugar and vanilla. Beat until creamy. Add eggs, one at a time, beating well after each addition. Gradually beat in flour mixture. Stir in 1 cup chocolate chips. Spread evenly into well-greased 15x10-inch jelly roll pan. Bake for 35 minutes. Remove from oven; sprinkle with remaining chocolate chips. Let stand for about 5 minutes until chips become shiny and soft. Spread evenly over top of brownies. Cool completely. Cut into squares.

Brownies

1/2 cup butter
1 cup sugar
4 eggs
2 tsp. vanilla

1 cup + 1 Tbsp. flour
1 can Hersheys chocolate syrup
chopped walnuts (optional)

Cream shortening and sugar. Add in eggs, one at a time. Add remaining ingredients and pour into greased (bottom only) jelly roll pan. Bake at 350 degrees for 25 minutes. Frost with Chocolate Brownie Frosting.

Rocky Road Fudge Bars

1/2 cup butter
1 square unsweetened chocolate
1 cup sugar
1 cup flour
Second layer:
6 oz. cream cheese
2 Tbsp. flour
1 egg
1/2 cup sugar

1/2 to 1 cup chopped nuts
1 tsp. baking powder
1 tsp. vanilla
2 eggs

1/4 cup soft butter
1/2 tsp. vanilla
1/2 cup nuts
6 oz. chocolate chips

Preheat oven to 350 degrees. Grease and flour 9x13 pan. In saucepan, over low heat, melt butter and chocolate. Add remaining first layer ingredients; mix well. Spread in prepared pan. In small bowl, combine second layer ingredients, except chopped nuts and chocolate chips. Mix well until smooth; add nuts and spread over chocolate mixture. Sprinkle chocolate chips on top. Bake 25-35 minutes. Sprinkle 2 cups mini marshmallows on top and bake 2 minutes longer.

In large pan, over low heat, melt: 1/4 cup butter, 1 square unsweetened chocolate, 1/4 cup milk, and 2 oz. cream cheese. Stir in: 3 cups powdered sugar and 1 tsp. vanilla. Stir until smooth. Immediately pour over marshmallows and swirl together. Makes 3 dozen bars.

Chocolate Chip Cookie Bars

2 1/4 cups flour
1 tsp. baking soda
1 tsp. salt
1 cup butter, softened
3/4 cup sugar

3/4 cup brown sugar, firmly packed
1 tsp. vanilla extract
2 eggs
12 oz. chocolate chips
1 cup chopped nuts

Preheat oven to 375 degrees. In small bowl, combine flour, baking soda and salt; set aside. In large bowl, combine butter, sugar, brown sugar, and vanilla; beat until creamy. Beat in eggs. Gradually add flour mixture; mix well. Stir in chocolate chips and nuts. Spread into greased 15x10-inch baking pan. Bake for 20-25 minutes. When cool, cut into 35 two-inch squares.

Chocolate Bars

1 cup sugar
1 cup brown sugar
1 cup margarine
2 eggs
2 cups flour

1 tsp. baking soda
3 cups oatmeal
6 oz. chocolate chips
1/2 cup margarine
14 oz. can sweetened condensed milk

Cream sugar, brown sugar and 1 cup margarine. Mix in eggs, flour, baking soda and oatmeal. Press 2/3 of the mixture into the bottom of an ungreased jelly roll pan. Over low heat, melt the chocolate chips, 1/2 cup margarine and milk. Pour that over the mixture in the pan and then cover with the remaining crumb mixture. Bake at 350 degrees for 25 minutes.

Cherry-Coconut Bars

1 cup flour
1/2 cup butter
3 Tbsp. confectioners' sugar
2 eggs, slightly beaten
1 cup sugar
1/4 cup flour

1/2 tsp. baking powder
1/4 tsp. salt
1 tsp. vanilla
3/4 cup chopped nuts
1/2 cup coconut
1/2 cup quartered maraschino cherries

Heat oven to 350 degrees. With hands, mix 1 cup flour, butter and confectioners' sugar until smooth. Spread thin with fingers in square pan, 8x8x2". Bake about 25 minutes. Stir all remaining ingredients into eggs. Spread over base. Bake about 25 minutes more. Cool. Makes twenty 3x1" bars. May also be cut into larger squares and served as dessert.

Cherry Dream Squares

1 pkg. white cake mix
1 1/4 cups rolled oats
1/2 cup margarine or butter, softened
1 egg

21 oz. can cherry pie filling
1/2 cup chopped nuts
1/4 cup packed brown sugar

Heat oven to 350 degrees. Grease 9x13 pan. In large bowl, combine cake mix, 6 Tbsp. margarine and 1 cup rolled oats. Mix until crumbly. Reserve 1 cup crumbs for top. To remaining crumbs, add 1 egg; mix until well blended. Press into prepared pan. Pour cherry pie filling over crust; spread to cover. To reserved crumbs, in large bowl, add remaining 1/4 cup rolled oats, 2 Tbsp. margarine, nuts and brown sugar. Beat until thoroughly mixed. Sprinkle over cherry filling. Bake 30-40 minutes or until golden brown. Cool completely before cutting. If desired, serve with a dollop of whipped cream.

Coconut Bars

25 graham crackers, crushed
1/2 cup +1/4 cup butter
1/4 cup sugar
14 oz. sweetened condensed milk

2 cups coconut
2 Tbsp. cream
6 Tbsp. brown sugar
powdered sugar

Mix graham cracker crumbs, 1/2 cup butter and sugar. Pat into 9x13 pan. Bake at 350 degrees for 10 minutes. Combine sweetened condensed milk and coconut. Pour into center of crust and spread out to sides. Bake an additional 10 minutes. Combine cream, 1/4 cup butter and brown sugar in saucepan; heat to boiling and boil 1 minute. Remove from heat; add powdered sugar until of spreading consistency. Spread over bars.

Apple Bars

2 1/2 cups + 1 Tbsp. flour
1 cup solid shortening
1 egg yolk + milk to make 2/3 cup
1/2 tsp. salt

1 1/2 cups crushed cornflakes
8 lbs. apples, peeled and sliced
2 tsp. cinnamon
1 cup sugar

Mix shortening, salt and 2 1/2 cups flour like pie crust; add milk and egg mixture. Form ball of dough. Divide dough in half; roll out one-half and put on cookie sheet with sides, putting dough up the sides. Spread crushed cornflakes on bottom of pan and add apples on top of cornflakes. Sprinkle 1 Tbsp. flour, cinnamon and sugar over the apples. Roll out other half of dough large enough to cover apples; fold sides over dough and press down lightly. Bake about 45 minutes at 350 degrees or until nice and brown. Frost with powdered sugar frosting.

Pumpkin Bars

4 eggs	2 tsp. baking powder
1 cup oil	1 tsp. baking soda
2 cups sugar	1/2 tsp. cloves
15 oz. canned pumpkin	1/2 tsp. salt
2 cups flour	1/2 tsp. ginger
2 tsp. cinnamon	1/2 tsp. nutmeg

Mix together well eggs, oil, sugar and pumpkin. Add remaining ingredients. Pour into greased and flour 12x8-inch pan (large cookie sheet) and bake 25-35 minutes at 350 degrees. When cool, frost with Cream Cheese Frosting.

Blarney Stones

3 egg yolks	1 1/2 tsp. baking powder
1 cup flour	1 tsp. vanilla
1/2 cup boiling water	1 egg yolks
4 egg whites	2 1/2 cups powdered sugar
1 cup sugar	1/2 cup butter or margarine, melted

Cream 3 egg yolks and sugar. Add flour and baking powder; mix. Add water and vanilla. Beat egg whites until stiff; fold into batter. Bake in jelly roll pan at 350 degrees for 15-20 minutes. To frost, combine 1 egg yolk, powdered sugar and melted butter. Mix with electric mixer. Top with salted sunflower nuts, if desired.

7 Layer Bars

1/2 cup margarine	1 cup coconut
1 1/2 cups graham cracker crumbs	1 cup nuts
12 oz. butterscotch chips	1 can sweetened condensed milk
12 oz. chocolate chips	

Melt margarine in 9x13 pan. Spread layers of graham crackers crumbs, butterscotch chips, chocolate chips, coconut and nuts, in that order. Drizzle sweetened condensed milk over the top. Bake at 300 degrees for 45 minutes to 1 hour, until brown.

Double Delicious Cookie Bars

1/2 cup margarine or butter
1 1/2 cups graham cracker crumbs
14 oz. can sweetened condensed milk

12 oz. chocolate chips
1 cup peanut butter chips

Preheat oven to 350 degrees. In a 9x13 baking pan, melt margarine in oven. Sprinkle crumbs over margarine; pour sweetened condensed milk over crumbs. Top with chips; press down firmly. Bake 25 to 30 minutes or until lightly browned. Cool. Cut into bars.

Club Cracker Bars

Club crackers
1/2 cup margarine
3/4 cup brown sugar
1/2 cup white sugar
1 cup crushed graham crackers

1/4 cup milk
2/3 cup peanut butter
1 cup chocolate chips (may be half
*   butterscotch chips, if desired)*

Line the bottom of a 9x13 pan with club crackers. Combine margarine, sugars, crushed graham crackers and milk. Bring to a boil and boil for 5 minutes. Pour over crackers and cover with another layer of club crackers. Melt together the chips and peanut butter. Spread over the top.

No Bake Butterscotch Peanut Butter Bars

2 eggs
1 cup sugar
3/4 cup butter
2 1/2 cups graham cracker crumbs
1/2 cup coconut

1/2 cup nutmeats
2 cups mini marshmallows
12 oz. butterscotch chips
3 Tbsp. peanut butter

Beat eggs; add sugar and butter. Bring to boil over low heat for 2 minutes. Let cool. When cool, add graham cracker crumbs, coconut, nutmeats and mini marshmallows. Press into 9x13" pan. Top with butterscotch chips, melted with peanut butter.

Can't Leave Alone Bars

1 white cake mix
1/3 cup oil
2 eggs

1/4 cup butter or margarine
1 can sweetened condensed milk
1 cup chocolate chips

Mix with fork: cake mix, oil and eggs. This mixture will form a ball like pizza dough. Pat half of the mixture into 9x13 cake pan, ungreased. Melt in saucepan: butter, condensed milk and chocolate chips. Pour over cake mixture and then put rest of cake mixture on top and swirl with knife. Bake at 350 degrees for 20 minutes. Rich, chewy and utterly delicious!! (Note: If you find it hard to spread the second half of the dough on top of the chocolate mixture, take little amounts of dough, about the size of a walnut, and pat it flat. Then carefully lay this over the filling. Repeat this procedure until all the dough is used. Then carefully swirl through the mixture with a knife.)

Heath Bars

soda crackers
1 cup brown sugar

1 cup butter
6 oz. chocolate chips

Line cookie side (with sides) with foil. Grease foil with a little butter and place soda crackers side by side on foil. Heat together brown sugar and butter. Stir well until butter is completely dissolved into sugar. Pour over crackers and bake at 400 degrees for 5 minutes. Remove from oven and sprinkle chocolate chips over the entire pan. Let stand until melted; spread like frosting. Sprinkle with chopped nuts, if desired.

Nut Goodie Bars

12 oz. chocolate chips
12 oz. butterscotch chips
2 cups peanut butter
1 cup salted peanuts
1/2 cup evaporated milk

1/4 cup vanilla pudding mix, not instant
1 cup butter
2 lb. powdered sugar
1 tsp. vanilla

Mix chips and peanut butter together and melt in saucepan. Pour a little less than half the mixture into a chilled jelly roll pan. Set remaining mixture aside and add salted peanuts. Mix together the evaporated milk, pudding mix and butter; bring to boiling and boil one minute. Remove from heat and add powdered sugar and vanilla. Blend well. Add to the first layer carefully. Chill 10 minutes. Spread remaining chocolate mixture on the top. Chill. Cut in small squares.

Oh Henry Bars

4 cups oatmeal
2/3 cup butter or margarine
1 cup brown sugar
1/2 cup white sugar

3 tsp. vanilla
12 oz. chocolate chips
1 cup crunchy peanut butter
chopped nuts (optional)

Mix oatmeal, butter, and sugars; press into buttered 9x13-inch pan. Bake 12 to 15 minutes at 350 degrees. Do not bake too long. Melt chocolate chips; add peanut butter and nuts. Pour over bars and spread frosting while still hot.

Good and Gooey Bars

14 oz. pkg. light caramels
1/3 cup evaporated milk
1 pkg. German Chocolate Cake mix
1 Tbsp. water

1/2 cup soft butter
1 cup chopped nuts
6 oz. chocolate chips

Flour and grease 9x13 pan. Combine the milk and caramels over low heat, stirring constantly. Set aside. Combine in large bowl the remaining ingredients except for the chocolate chips. Stir with fork until dough is crumbly but holds together. Put half of the mixture in the cake pan and bake at 350 degrees for 6 minutes. Put chocolate chips over the baked crust. Spread caramel mixture over that. Cover with remainder of dough mixture and bake at 350 degrees for 15-20 minutes. Cut in smaller portions as this is quite rich.

Prayer Bars

1/2 cup melted butter
4 Tbsp. cocoa
1/2 cup powdered sugar
1 tsp. vanilla
Second Layer:
1/2 cup butter
1 Tbsp. milk

1 egg
1/2 cup chopped nuts
1 cup coconut
2 cups graham cracker crumbs

2 Tbsp. vanilla pudding mix (not instant)
2 cups powdered sugar

For first layer, mix melted butter, cocoa and powdered sugar. Add remaining first layer ingredients. Press into 9x13 pan and refrigerate. For second layer, mix in saucepan: butter, milk and pudding mix. Cook until thick, stirring constantly. Cool. Add powdered sugar; mix until smooth and spread over first layer. Refrigerate or put in freezer for a few minutes. Melt over water in double boiler 1 giant (8 oz.) Hershey chocolate bar. Spread over second layer in pan. Let sit at room temperature; cut, then refrigerate.

Special K Bars

2/3 cup light corn syrup
2/3 cup sugar
1 tsp. vanilla
1 cup old fashioned peanut butter

Special K cereal
6 oz. chocolate chips
6 oz. butterscotch chips
1 tsp. butter

Combine syrup, and sugar; bring to a boil and add vanilla. Add peanut butter; stir until smooth. Add cereal until thick. Spread in greased pan. Melt together the chips and butter and spread over bars.

Toffee Bars

1 cup butter
1 cup brown sugar
1 egg yolk
2 cups flour

10 - 1 oz. Hershey bars (or 10 oz.
    milk chocolate chips)
1/2 cup chopped nuts

In saucepan, melt butter; stir in brown sugar and egg yolk. Add flour and pour into 9x13 greased pan. Bake for 20 minutes at 350 degrees. When hot, place candy bars over toffee mixture to melt; spread chocolate evenly over the top. Sprinkle nuts over chocolate. Let cool and cut into bars.

Caramel Bars

32 caramels
1 cup flour
3/4 cup brown sugar
1/4 tsp. salt
1/2 cup chocolate chips

5 Tbsp. evaporated milk or cream
1 cup oatmeal
1/2 tsp. soda
3/4 cup butter, melted
1/2 cup chopped nuts

Melt caramels and milk in double boiler. Combine other ingredients except chocolate, nuts, and caramel sauce. Stir until all butter is absorbed and mixture is crumbly. Press half of crumbs in 9x9-inch pan. Bake at 350 degrees for 8 to 10 minutes. Remove from oven. Sprinkle on chips and nuts. Pour caramel sauce evenly over chips. Sprinkle on remaining crumbs. Bake 12 to 15 minutes. Cut while warm.

Caramel Nut Bars

2 cups flour
3/4 cup brown sugar, packed
1 egg, beaten
3/4 cup margarine or butter

3/4 cup chopped walnuts
24 caramels, unwrapped
14 oz. sweetened condensed milk

Preheat oven to 350 degrees. In large bowl, combine flour, sugar, and egg; cut in 1/2 cup margarine until crumbly. Stir in walnuts. Reserving 2 cups crumb mixture, press remainder firmly on bottom of greased 9x13" pan. Bake 15 minutes. Meanwhile, in heavy saucepan (T-Fal works great), over low heat, melt caramels with sweetened condensed milk and remaining 1/4 cup margarine. Pour over prepared crust. Top with reserved crumb mixture. Bake 20 minutes or until bubbly. Cool; cut into bars.

Oatmeal Fudge Bars

1/2 cup shortening
1 cup brown sugar
1 egg
1/2 tsp. vanilla
3/4 cup flour
1/2 tsp. baking soda
1/2 tsp. salt

2 cups quick-cook oats
6 oz. chocolate chips
2 Tbsp. butter
1/3 cup condensed milk or cream
1/4 tsp. salt
1 tsp. vanilla

Cream together shortening, brown sugar, egg, 1/2 tsp. vanilla; blend in flour, soda, 1/2 tsp. salt, and oats. Reserve one cup of mixture for top. Press remainder into greased 9x13 pan. Combine chocolate chips, butter, condensed milk, 1/4 tsp. salt and 1 tsp. vanilla. Melt together until chocolate chips are melted. Spread over oatmeal layer and sprinkle with reserved oatmeal mixture. Bake 25 minutes at 350 degrees.

Graham Squares

graham cracker squares
1 cup brown sugar
1 cup coconut

1/3 cup milk
1/2 cup butter

Line a 9x13-inch pan with graham cracker squares. Combine brown sugar, coconut, milk and butter in saucepan; bring to boil and boil for 8 minutes. Pour over graham crackers in pan and top with another layer of graham cracker squares. Frost with powdered sugar frosting.

Easy Lemon Bars

1 pkg. of one-step angel food cake mix   *1 can lemon pie filling*

With a spoon, stir together cake mix and pie filling. Pour into ungreased jelly roll pan and bake 20-25 minutes in 350 degree oven. When cool, frost with powdered sugar frosting flavored with lemon extract. This freezes well.

Lemon Bars Deluxe

2 cups flour   *2 cups sugar*
1/2 cup powdered sugar   *1/3 cup lemon juice*
1 cup margarine   *1/4 cup flour*
4 beaten eggs   *1/2 tsp. baking powder*

Mix 2 cups flour, powdered sugar and margarine until crumbled. Press into bottom and part-way up sides of a 9x13-inch pan. Bake at 350 degrees until lightly browned, about 20-25 minutes. Beat eggs, sugar and lemon juice. Add 1/4 cup flour and baking powder. Pour over crust. Bake 25 minutes. Sprinkle with powdered sugar.

Lemon Love Notes

1/2 cup margarine   *2 Tbsp. flour*
1 cup flour   *1/2 tsp. baking powder*
1/4 cup powdered sugar   *2 Tbsp. lemon juice*
2 eggs, slightly beaten   *grated lemon rind (optional)*
1 cup sugar

Mix margarine, 1 cup flour and powdered sugar and press into 8 inch square pan. Bake 15 minutes at 325 degrees. Cool. Mix remaining ingredients; pour over baked mixture and bake again 20-25 minutes at 350 degrees. Cool. Frost with lemon frosting.

Grandma Ruby's Lemon Bars

2 eggs
1 1/2 cups sugar
2 Tbsp. water
juice and rind of two lemons
1/2 cup butter

1/2 cup brown sugar, packed
1 cup flour
1/2 tsp. soda
1/2 cup grated coconut
20 squares soda crackers, crushed

Beat eggs; add 1 cup sugar, water, juice and rind of lemons. Mix and cook until slightly thickened. Cool. In a separate bowl, mix together remaining ingredients, including the remaining 1/2 cup of sugar. Reserve 3/4 cup of mixture for topping; pat crust into ungreased 9x13 pan. Pour lemon filling over crust. Sprinkle remaining crust over the top. Bake at 350 degrees for 30 minutes. NOTE: Do not put lemon filling all the way to the edge, as it will burn to sides.

Lemon Layer Bars

2 cups flour
1 cup butter, softened
1/2 cup powdered sugar
4 eggs, beaten

4 Tbsp. lemon juice
1 tsp. baking powder
2 cups sugar
4 Tbsp. flour

Mix 2 cups flour, butter and powdered sugar. Pat into 10x15-inch pan. Bake at 350 degrees for 15 minutes. Blend remaining ingredients; pour over crust and bake 20 minutes or until light brown. Cool. Frost with powdered sugar.

Raisin Bars

1 cup raisins
2 cups water
1/2 cup shortening
1 cup sugar
1 3/4 cups flour

1/2 tsp. salt
1 tsp. soda
1 tsp. cinnamon
1/2 tsp. nutmeg
1/2 cup chopped walnuts (optional)

Boil raisins and water together for 10 minutes. Add shortening and cool. Add remaining ingredients and pour into 9x13 baking pan. Bake in 350 degree oven for 25 minutes. Frost with caramel frosting.

Puppy Chow

12 oz. chocolate chips
12 oz. butterscotch chips
1 tsp. butter

1 large box Crispix cereal
powdered sugar

Melt chocolate chips, butterscotch chips and butter until smooth. Pour chocolate mixture over cereal and mix well. Pour powdered sugar over cereal, cover, and shake mixture to coat with the powdered sugar. Repeat until well coated. Kids love this!

Peppermint Candy

8-9 medium size candy canes, crushed
1 lb. white chocolate

red food coloring, if desired

Melt white chocolate over double boiler; stir in crushed candy cane chips. Add red food coloring, if desired. Spread mixture thinly on greased cookie sheet or foil. Cool. Cut or break into pieces for serving.

Easter Egg Nests

6 oz. white almond bark
1 1/3 cup flaked coconut
1/2 tsp. milk

green food coloring
1 bag tiny jelly beans

In a small mixing bowl, stir together a few drops of food coloring and the milk. Add the coconut and stir until it is evenly tinted; set aside. Place the almond bark in a 4 cup measure. Microwave until almond bark is melted. Watch closely and stir often. Mix the tinted coconut in with melted almond bark. Place a spoonful of the mixture on wax paper. Shape into little nests. Makes about 12 nests. After they have cooled, place 4 or 5 jelly beans in the center of each nest.

Peanut Brittle

1 cup white corn syrup
2 cups sugar
1/2 cup water
12 oz. peanuts

2 Tbsp. butter
2 tsp. vanilla
2 tsp. soda
1/2 tsp. salt

Combine syrup, sugar and water in saucepan. Heat slowly to 230 degrees. Add peanuts and continue to cook, stirring constantly, until at 300 degrees. Remove from heat and add butter, vanilla, salt and soda. Mix well and pour into well buttered jelly roll pan, 15x10-inch. Break into pieces when cooled.

Peanut Butter Cups

1/3 cup peanut butter
1/4 cup powdered sugar
1 tsp. vanilla

8 oz. chocolate almond bark
1/2 cup peanut butter

Blend 1/3 cup peanut butter, powdered sugar and vanilla. Form into small balls and put in paper candy cups. Chill, if desired (not really necessary.) Melt almond bark and 1/2 cup peanut butter. Pour over peanut butter balls. Chill.

Easy Peanut Butter Chocolate Fudge

12 oz. pkg. peanut butter chips
14 oz. sweetened condensed milk
1/4 cup butter or margarine

1/2 cup chopped peanuts
6 oz. chocolate chips

In large saucepan, melt peanut butter , 1 cup of sweetened condensed milk and 2 Tbsp. butter; stir occasionally. Remove from heat; stir in peanuts. Spread mixture into wax paper-lined 8x8-inch pan. In small saucepan, melt chocolate chips, remaining sweetened condensed milk and butter. Spread chocolate mixture on top of peanut butter mixture. Chill two hours or until firm. Turn fudge onto cutting board; peel off paper and cut into squares. Tightly cover any leftovers.

Snicker Snacks

graham cracker squares
3/4 cup butter
3/4 cup packed brown sugar

1 cup or more chocolate chips
1 cup salted peanuts (optional)

Place graham crackers side by side in an ungreased jelly roll pan. In saucepan, combine butter and brown sugar and cook over medium heat, stirring occasionally, until mixture comes to a boil, about 3 to 5 minutes. Boil 5 minutes, stirring constantly. Immediately pour over graham crackers and spread evenly. Sprinkle with the chocolate chips. Let stand until melted, about 1 minute; then spread. Sprinkle with peanuts and lightly press into chocolate. Cool and break into pieces.

Butterscotch Pillows

1 cup white sugar
1/2 cup brown sugar
1/3 cup white corn syrup

1/3 cup butter
1/2 cup heavy cream
1/2 cup chopped pecans

Mix together all ingredients, except nuts. Bring to boil and cook, stirring constantly, until a little tried in water will form a ball. Add chopped nuts. Turn into a buttered cake or jelly roll pan. When cool, shape into little bite-sized pillows, roll in powdered sugar, and wrap in waxed paper. Enjoy!

Penoche

2 cups brown sugar
1 Tbsp. white corn syrup
3/4 cup milk

1 tsp. butter
1 tsp. vanilla
chopped nuts

Mix brown sugar, syrup and milk; boil to fairly hard ball stage. Remove from heat and add butter and vanilla. Beat with electric mixer; add nuts and pour onto buttered dish.

English Toffee

1/2 cup butter	nuts
1/2 cup sugar	chocolate

Butter a pie pan or shallow pan. Cover bottom with coarsely chopped nuts. In a heavy pan, cook butter and sugar until golden brown; spread over nuts. Sprinkle top with chocolate chips or Hershey bar squares. Let chocolate melt to form a layer over candy. Then sprinkle more nuts on top.

Buttery Caramels

1 cup butter	1 cup corn syrup
2 1/4 cups brown sugar	14 oz. sweetened condensed milk
dash of salt	1 tsp. vanilla

Melt butter in heavy saucepan. Add brown sugar and salt; stir thoroughly. Add corn syrup; mix well and gradually add sweetened condensed milk, stirring constantly over medium heat until candy reaches firm ball stage (245 degrees), about 15 to 20 minutes. Remove from heat and stir in vanilla. Pour into a buttered 9x9 or 9x13-inch pan. When cooled, cut and wrap pieces with wax paper.

Quick Turtles

1 1/2 cups pecan halves	5 bars milk chocolate (1 1/2 oz. each),
14 oz.pkg. vanilla caramels, unwrapped	broken into squares

Arrange pecans in clusters of 3 or 4 halves, 2 inches apart, on a greased baking pan. Top each cluster with 1 caramel, flattened slightly. Bake at 300 degrees for 7 minutes or until caramel softens. Remove to wax paper. Flatten caramels with spatula, top each candy with 1 milk chocolate square while still warm. Spread chocolate when melted. Refrigerate a few minutes until chocolate hardens.

Marshmallow Candy

1 German chocolate bar
2 Tbsp. butter
1 egg
1 cup powdered sugar

1 cup chopped nuts
10 oz. miniature marshmallows,
    colored preferred
coconut

Melt chocolate bar and butter in a double boiler. Beat in egg and powdered sugar. Add nuts and marshmallows. Put on waxed paper; shape into log shape. Freeze and slice. The log can be rolled in coconut.

Divinity

3 cups sugar
1/2 cup white corn syrup
1/8 tsp. salt
2/3 cup water

2 egg whites
1 tsp. vanilla
1 cup chopped nuts

Boil sugar, syrup and water to fairly hard ball stage. Beat egg whites and salt in the meantime. Pour syrup slowly into egg whites with mixer going at moderate speed. Continue to beat until gloss disappears and candy is ready to drop. Add vanilla and nuts. Drop by teaspoonfuls onto waxed paper.

Fudge

4 1/2 cups sugar
13 oz. evaporated milk
9 oz. semi-sweet chocolate chips
9 oz. bittersweet chocolate chips

7 oz. marshmallow cream
1/2 lb. butter
1 Tbsp. vanilla
2 cups chopped walnuts

Bring sugar and milk to a boil and cook exactly 6 minutes over medium heat. Remove from stove and add remaining ingredients. Beat until firm. Pour into 9x13 pan, greased. Cool to room temperature, then store overnight in refrigerator. Makes 5 lbs. candy.

E-Z Fudge

1 can sweetened condensed milk
12 oz. pkg. chocolate chips
12 oz. pkg. butterscotch chips
1 cup miniature marshmallows

1/2 tsp. salt
3/4 cup chopped nuts
1 1/2 tsp. vanilla

Melt the chips with the sweetened condensed milk. Stir in vanilla, salt and nuts. Add the marshmallows and stir. Pour into greased pans (two 8x8" or one 9x13".) Chill and set. Makes 1 1/2 pounds of fudge.

Chocolate Fudge

12 oz. semi-sweet chocolate chips
6 oz. milk chocolate chips
14 oz. sweetened condensed milk

dash of salt
1/2 to 1 cup chopped nuts
1 1/2 tsp. vanilla extract

Over low heat, melt chips with sweetened condensed milk and salt. Remove from heat and stir in nuts and vanilla. Spread evenly into waxpaper-lined 8 or 9-inch square pan. Chill two hours or until firm. Turn fudge onto cutting board, peel off paper and cut into squares. Store at room temperature.

Potato Candy

1 lb. powdered sugar
8 oz. coconut
2/3 cup mashed potatoes

1 cup chocolate chips
1 tsp. white corn syrup

Combine powdered sugar, coconut and mashed potatoes; mix until smooth. Spread in a greased 8 or 9-inch square pan. Melt chocolate chips and add corn syrup. Spread over potato mixture. Chill for two hours. Cut into squares.

"Irish Potatoes"

1 cup confectioner's sugar
1 cup shredded coconut

1 1/2 Tbsp. half-and-half
cinnamon

Sprinkle the sugar on the coconut. Add half-and-half and mix gently. Scoop by 1/2 tablespoons and knead into balls. Place cinnamon in small pastic bag and shake "potatoes" in cinnamon until coated. (This recipe was given to me by Karen Kennedy. The recipe is from Kilkenny County, between Tipperary and Wexford in Southern Ireland, where Karen Kennedy's family resided.)

QVC

One of the best things I ever did concerning my career was to accept the job offered to me by QVC when the merger between CVN and QVC took place. Like any new job, it was scary and there were lots of adjustments. The hardest part was moving the family to Pennsylvania, away from our parents and siblings, but, as in everything, you adjust, draw closer together and make new friends in new surroundings. QVC's staff was very friendly and helpful about getting me acclimated to everything. My time at QVC has definitely been a time of learning. I think I've done as much reading and studying in the last few years as I ever did when I was in college. But, the more I learn, the more I realize there's so much more to learn.

I truly love my job! I look forward to going to work each and every day. I love talking to the viewers and getting feedback from them. I love the people I work with and respect them all a lot for the abilities they have.

Of course, a highlight of my job is meeting all the special guests with whom I've worked. My friend, Bette Ball, is always so kind and generous. She and her husband, George, have become close, personal friends of ours. Lee Sands is a wonderful friend and a man I respect a lot. Virginia Olson is such a joy. I've also enjoyed working with celebrities such as Nolan Miller, a true professional and a very kind and gentle man; Marie Osmond, a genuine friend whose care and concern for others overwhelms me; Annette Funicello, one of the sweetest ladies I've ever met, who truly loves life; Linda Dano, classy from top to bottom but so down-to-earth and real; other celebrities with whom I've had the privilege of working include Tova Borgnine, Susan Lucci, George Hamilton, Richard Simmons, Joan Rivers, Gary Collins, Candy Spelling, Victoria Principal, Rue McClanahan, Phyllis George, and Sally Jesse Raphael.

It"s always been a pleasure to work with these people who have worked so hard to get their products developed and are so excited to be on QVC.

All in all, QVC is such an exciting place to be with all the innovative changes, new products going forward, and all the new viewers shopping with QVC. I consider it to be a real privilege to get paid to do something I absolutely love!

Eric and Cory are both so thrilled with the "Eric" and "Cory" dolls designed by Bette Ball. They love to come "on air" and always enjoy their time on the school set at QVC!

Marie Osmond

Richard Simmons

GOOD FRIENDS

SPECIAL PEOPLE

Bette Ball

Annette Funicello

Nolan Miller

Lee Sands

Phyllis George

I love to meet the viewers!

Miscellaneous

Caramel Popcorn

6 cups popped corn
2 Tbsp. margarine or butter

2 Tbsp. honey

Spread the popcorn evenly in baking pan. In saucepan, melt the margarine or butter and honey. Pour over popcorn, stirring to coat all pieces. Bake at 325 degrees for 8-10 minutes, stirring often. Cool.

Caramel Corn

10 cups popped corn
1 1/2 cup peanuts
1/2 cup butter
1 cup brown sugar, packed

1 cup dark corn syrup
1/4 tsp. salt
1/4 tsp. baking soda
1/2 tsp. vanilla

Mix popcorn and peanuts. In a saucepan, combine butter, brown sugar, corn syrup and salt. Bring to a boil, stirring constantly. Boil 5 minutes. Remove from heat. Add baking soda and vanilla. Pour over popped corn and peanuts. Stir. Bake at 250 degrees for 45 minutes, stirring every 15 minutes.

Honey Butter

16 oz. creamy clover honey

1 lb. butter

Beat the butter and honey together until fluffy. Regular honey will work too, but if you can find this creamy white kind, it is better.

Christmas Apple Jelly

1 quart apple juice
5 drops red food coloring

1 3/4 oz. pkg. powdered fruit pectin
5 1/2 cups sugar

Combine apple juice, food coloring and powdered fruit pectin in large saucepan. Bring mixture to full boil, then stir in sugar until it dissolves. Bring to boil again and let boil for 2 minutes. Take from heat, skim if necessary. Pour into hot sterilized jars and seal. Yield: 7 half-pints. This makes a nice Christmas gift when you have lots of parties and want to take a unique gift.

Curried Fruit

1 can pineapple slices
1 can pear halves
Maraschino cherries

2/3 cup brown sugar
1/3 cup butter
2 tsp. curry powder

Drain pineapple slices and pear halves, and set on paper towel to completely drain. Place pineapple slices in baking pan, and put pear halves on top of pineapple slices. Add cherries on top of pears for color. Melt together the brown sugar and butter and curry powder. Pour over fruit and bake uncovered at 350 degrees for 45 minutes.

Broiled Grapefruit

Sprinkle grapefruit halves with cinnamon and brown sugar. Dot with butter or margarine. Broil 10 minutes.

Poached Pears

1/2 cup sugar
1/2 cup water
1/4 cup lemon juice

3-4 large pears
1 cinnamon stick

Poach 30 minutes on stove or 45-60 minutes in 350 degree oven, covered. Cool. Garnish with raspberries or blackberries and serve on a bed of whipped cream.

Dad's Pancake/Waffle Syrup

1 cup powdered sugar
1 cup brown sugar
1 cup sugar
1/4 cup flour

4 cups water
1/4 lb. butter
1 tsp. vanilla

Combine all ingredients, except butter and vanilla, in saucepan and slow boil to thicken; then add butter and vanilla. Serve warm.

Knox Blox

4 envelopes Knox unflavored gelatin
9 oz. jello, any flavor

4 cups boiling water

Dissolve gelatins in boiling water. Pour into pan and chill. Cut into squares or use cookie cutters to make forms.

Barbeque Sauce

1 cup ketchup
1/4 cup Worcestershire sauce
1 cup water
1/4 cup vinegar

1 Tbsp. sugar
1 tsp. salt
1/2 tsp. celery salt
2 Tbsp. minced onion

Cook to blend flavors and onion. May be brushed on grilled hamburgers or poured over browned meat and baked. Good also for ribs.

Barbeque Sauce

1 onion, chopped
1 green pepper, chopped (optional)
3/4 cup cold water
1 cup ketchup
2 Tbsp. vinegar

2 Tbsp. Worcestershire sauce
2 Tbsp. lemon juice
3 Tbsp. brown sugar
1 tsp. dry mustard
salt and pepper to taste

Simmer for 20 minutes or microwave for 5 minutes.

Hot Fudge Sauce

1 1/4 cup chocolate chips
1/2 cup + 2 Tbsp. margarine
13 oz. can evaporated milk

2 1/2 cups powdered sugar
1 1/4 tsp. vanilla

Melt chips and margarine; add sugar, vanilla and milk, blending well. Bring to a boil, stirring constantly. Cook about 8 minutes.

Thick 'N' Rich Hot Fudge Sauce

4 (1 ounce) squares semi-sweet chocolate   14 oz. sweetened condensed milk
2 Tbsp. butter or margarine   1 tsp. vanilla extract
dash salt

In medium saucepan, over low heat, melt chocolate and butter; stir in remaining ingredients. Cook, stirring constantly, about 5 minutes or until mixture is slightly thickened. Makes 1 2/3 cups. Refrigerate leftovers. To reheat, combine sauce with a small amount of water; heat slowly, stirring constantly, over low heat.

Marshmallow Fudge Topping

1 cup brown sugar   1 Tbsp. butter
1/4 cup cocoa   1 tsp. vanilla
1/2 cup milk   1 cup miniature marshmallows

Mix brown sugar and cocoa in one-quart saucepan. Stir in milk. Cook and stir until mixture comes to boiling. Cook rapidly five minutes longer. Remove from heat and stir in butter and vanilla. Cool five minutes and fold in marshmallows. Makes about 1 1/4 cups sauce. Serve warm over vanilla ice cream.

So-Delicious Chocolate Sauce

10 oz. marshmallows   dash of salt
1/2 cup evaporated milk   1 tsp. vanilla
3 (1 oz.) squares unsweetened chocolate

Heat marshmallows and milk in double boiler until marshmallows melt, stirring occasionally. Add chocolate and stir until smooth. Blend in salt and vanilla. Serve warm over ice cream.

Pickled Beets

3/4 cup vinegar
1/2 cup water
scant 3/4 cup sugar
1/2 tsp. allspice

3/4" stick whole cinnamon
1/8 tsp. whole cloves
1/4 tsp. salt

If fresh beets are used, cook until just tender. Slip skins. Combine the above ingredients and bring to a boil; simmer for 15 minutes. Put beets in jar; pour mixture over. Cool and refrigerate.

Pickles

25-30 cucumbers, sliced
8 large onions, sliced
2 large peppers, sliced
1/2 cup canning salt

5 cups vinegar
5 cups sugar
2 Tbsp. mustard seed
1 tsp. tumeric

Combine sliced cucumbers, onions and peppers with salt. Set aside for 3 hours; drain. Boil remaining ingredients; add cucumbers, onions and peppers. Heat through but do not boil. Pack and seal.

Dill Pickles

8 1/3 cups water
4 cups vinegar
2/3 cup salt
sugar

dill
garlic
cucumbers
alum lumps

Combine water, vinegar and salt; boil 15 minutes. Put cucumbers, dill and garlic in jars; put 1 Tbsp. sugar in each jar and add vinegar mixture to fill. Add one pea size lump alum to each jar. Boil and seal each jar. Wait at least 8 weeks before using.

Russian Dills

cucumbers in slices, long
3 Tbsp. salt
2 cups sugar

1 1/2 cups water
2 cups vinegar
garlic & dill

Put cucumber slices in jars. Combine salt, sugar, water and vinegar; boil. Pour over cucumbers; add garlic and dill to each jar. Seal.

Good Smooth Playdough

2 cups flour
1 cup salt
2 cups water

2 Tbsp. cooking oil
4 tsp. cream of tartar
food coloring

Cook ingredients in sauce pan until stiff and lumpy. Dump out onto waxed paper. Knead until it reaches playdough consistency.

Homemade Fingerpaints

2 cups plastic liquid starch

1 cup Ivory Snow flakes

Beat with rotary beater or electric mixer until the volume is tripled. Divide and add food coloring as desired. Store in covered containers in refrigerator. Freezer paper is good for painting on. Wet waxy side of paper slightly; then put a spoonful of paint on the paper and have a wonderful, messy adventure!

Make-Up (for Halloween)

2 tsp. white shortening
5 tsp. cornstarch
1 tsp. flour

3 to 4 drops glycerin
food coloring

Mix ingredients together like paste. Add colorings.

APPRECIATION TO VIEWERS

I want to express my sincere appreciation and gratitude to all of the QVC viewers who have watched my shows, who have written to me, spoken with me on the phone over the TV, sent me recipes, tidbits of information, photos, or little gifts. I have a close family, but I also feel that I have an extended family with the people who have been so kind to me through QVC. Some of you have been with me since my CVN days, and some of you may be new to QVC. Either way, I'm always concerned that each of you is satisfied with your purchases and that there are no surprises when you receive your purchases.

I do hope you continue to watch QVC, learn new and interesting tidbits of information, laugh with us when unexpected things happen on "live" TV, and continue to say "Hi" on the phone during my shows. Keep those cards and letters coming so I know what's going on in your life.

Thank you for all of your support! Enjoy my cookbook!!

With Love from the Roes

INDEX

INDEX

INDEX

INDEX

INDEX